ANYAN'S STORY

A New Guinea Woman

in Two Worlds

ANYAN'S STORY
A New Guinea Woman
in Two Worlds

Virginia Drew Watson

A McLellan Book

University of Washington Press

Seattle and London

This book is published with the assistance of a grant from the
McLellan Endowed Series Fund, established through the generosity
of Martha McCleary McLellan and Mary McLellan Williams.

Library of Congress Cataloging-in-Publication Data

Watson, Virginia.
Anyan's story : a New Guinea woman in two worlds /
Virginia Drew Watson.
p.　cm.
"A McLellan book."
Includes bibliographical references and index.
ISBN 0-295-97589-X (alk. paper) (cl.)
0-295-97604-7 (pbk.)
1. Anyan.　2. Women, Tairora—Biography.　3. Women, Tairora—
Social conditions.　4. Women, Tairora—Cultural assimilation.
5. Tairora (Papua New Guinea people)—Social life and customs.
6. Kainantu (Papua New Guinea)—Social life and customs.
I. Title.
DU740.42.W38　　1997　　96-42573
995.3—dc20

Contents

Preface

THREE DECADES HAVE ELAPSED SINCE ANYAN AND I WERE together. There has been time to assess the flexibility and resilience of this one person during her passage from life in a culture in which metal tools were unknown to life in a society where advanced technology was a given. The brief temporal span of the great cultural distance traveled is notable. Uncommon in its proximity to the actual journey, this is the story of one of many individuals who have experienced the shock of cultural transplantation. Whatever the space or time, some of those who were forced to make the move from one culture to another were consumed by it, and some were consigned to straddling the dark void that the cultural disparities created. Others, like Anyan, were able to maintain equilibrium in both cultures.

The story is set among a people called Tairora who live in the highlands of New Guinea, the large island north of Australia. The country is currently known as Papua New Guinea; at the time of the fieldwork that my husband James B. Watson and I undertook, the official name of a somewhat differently defined country was United Nations Trust Territory of New Guinea. In this monograph I shall use Papua New Guinea and New Guinea, as well as Papua New Guineans and New Guineans, interchangeably. The Tairora are one of several groups—Gadsup, Agarabi, and Kamano are the others—who occupy a circumscribed area in the very eastern section of the highlands. They are people who speak languages that, although related to one another, are not mutually intelligible. In other respects—material culture, social practices, supernatural beliefs—they share similarities, not identities.

Anyan was born at a time when the Tairora were still living in what is stereotypically called the Stone Age, a term that reflects a

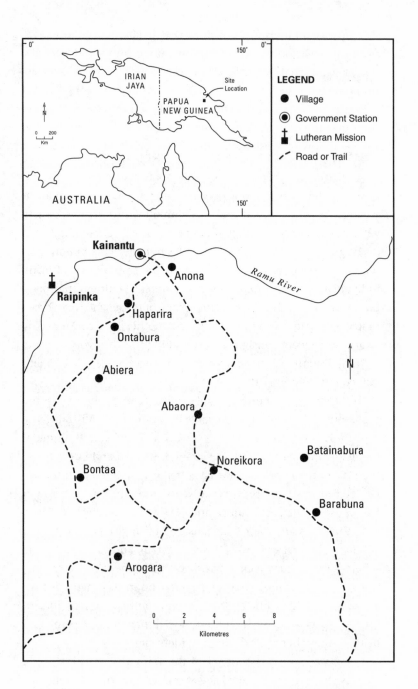

0°

150°

0°

150°

IRIAN JAYA

PAPUA NEW GUINEA

Site Location

N

0   200
Km

AUSTRALIA

Kainantu

Anona

Ramu River

✝
■ **Raipinka**

●
Haparira

●
Ontabura

●
Abiera

●
Abaora

●
Batainabura

●
Noreikora

●
Bontaa

●
Barabuna

N

●
Arogara

0   2   4   6   8

Kilometres

dependence on tools made of stone and an absence of those made of metal. That tools made of bamboo, bone, and wood were also used suggests that "non-metal" or "pre-metal" might be more appropriate terms.

While Anyan was still a child, new cultural influences began to filter into the highlands of Papua New Guinea. The putative date for the inflow of Westerners, their ideas, behaviors, and values is 1930. Their early impact on the local population was sporadic, sometimes halting, in no way a steady pulse, let alone a torrent. It was broken temporarily during World War II, after which Westernization increased in intensity. What is now the town of Kainantu, the "Station," was the seat of law and order, Western style, for the region, and a focal point for the dissemination of Western influence.

During our initial eighteen-month experience in Papua New Guinea, we lived and worked in several eastern highlands villages.[1] One of them was the Tairora hamlet of Haparira. Here, as in other Tairora villages, women spoke only their native language. Because I was not yet familiar with the Tairora language, I needed an interpreter, someone who could communicate in a language that she and I shared. As I intended to work almost exclusively with women, a female interpreter was preferable. This presented an almost insurmountable problem because at that time, among thousands of Tairora, there were no women who knew English and very few who spoke what was then called Melanesian Pidgin. The current term for the latter is Tok Pisin; it refers to one of two national languages of Papua New Guinea.

Word of my need filtered into Kainantu, where Anyan resided. One day she came to our house and expressed a desire to be my *tanim tok* ("a person who turns one language into another"). She could turn her language, Tairora, into Tok Pisin, the language she and I shared. Anyan would live in her native village, Abiera, a community within walking distance of our residence. She preferred this arrangement to living with us because it would give her an opportunity to spend more time with her elderly father, with other relatives, and with old friends.

She was glad, too, for the opportunity to give her children a taste of village life—of life lived among a bevy of caring, nurturing kinsmen. This was absent in the Station life in which the children were growing up, where the local subculture was an amalgam of cultural residues from various parts of Papua New Guinea, brought together by policemen, medical orderlies, cargo handlers—men engaged in work for the government or other Westerners—and their families.

The prospect looked propitious. Not only was Anyan acquainted with the people among whom we were living and their culture but her command of Tok Pisin was excellent. We arrived at a mutually satisfactory arrangement, attested to, I believe, by the fact that it endured for so long.

My field notes, the single source of what follows, were not collected with the intention of writing Anyan's life history. My fieldwork focused on the roles of women in relation to family structure in the two ethnolinguistic groups among whom we lived and worked, the Agarabi and Tairora. My doctoral dissertation, "Agarabi Female Roles and Family Structure" (University of Chicago, 1965), is based on data that I collected among the Agarabi.

During our conversations together or with Tairora women, Anyan often alluded to events in her own life that she thought would interest me or help to clarify a particular problem I might be struggling with, such as an elusive point in the kinship system. Her comments were interspersed randomly throughout my notebooks. Toward the end of our second period of fieldwork in 1964, I realized that although none of the data was solicited or selected for the purpose of writing a biography, I had accumulated information about Anyan that could be used to weave a tapestry of one life.

When I told her this she was elated. She immediately perceived its relevance to telling the story of her people as they lived before Western culture overtook them and they changed in their attempt to accept the rather awful forces that impinged on them. She was anxious that everyone know about Tairora. Her pride in her upbringing, in her culture, in her beautiful corner of the world, was apparent. She seemed to assume responsibility for describing and explaining her people and culture to those unfamiliar with them. In fact, she expressed more excitement than I had seen her evince in our entire time together. I knew Anyan as a fairly placid, even-tempered person—a result, perhaps, of the personality modification that accompanies acculturation.

My choice of Anyan about whom to write was to some extent fortuitous. In contrast to many subjects of biographies written by anthropologists, she was not chosen because of her indubitable position of leadership in her community. To what extent she was outstanding among her Tairora peers can be deduced at least partly from her selection at an early age from the youth of her village, both male and female, to move to a village not far from Kainantu to learn Tok Pisin. This would enable her to act as interpreter for her people, among whom there were no speakers of the language. A few years later, when contemplating a move to Kainantu, she was encouraged by her superiors to go so that she could continue to increase her proficiency in the language. For several years thereafter she served as interpreter between the Tairora and the governmental functionaries.

It will be clear, I believe, that this account is not a structured life history with a specified point of view or intellectual thrust. It partakes of history, psychology, sociology, anthropology, and humanity in suggesting the interplay of forces, subtle and dynamic, that affected the life of one individual as she moved from the world of the bark raiment of her youth to the cotton wardrobe of her adulthood.

This account is a new creation. Our conversations were conducted in Tok Pisin heavily larded with Tairora words and phrases. The multilanguage cast of the data poses some problems. Translating directly from Tok Pisin renders stilted English, more hindrance than help to the reader. On the other hand, an approximation to standard—not to mention elegant—English would be inappropriate in the sense of substantial loss of the general feel and tenor of the way the events I am reporting were relayed to me. I have chosen to write in rather inelegant standard English. In the interest of clarity and ease of reading I have taken steps to organize the material, altering the style in which it was related. At the same time I have tried to retain something of the cadence, especially for Anyan's early years—short, choppy sentences, a limited vocabulary, and much repetition, all transmitted in a rather low key.

As Anyan and I worked together our schedule was flexible and our activities varied from day to day. On some days work was fairly intensive, and on others Anyan could spend time with her friends in the village. One aspect of Western culture already implanted in her was the five-day work week. Unless something of importance was planned for Saturday or Sunday, she spent weekends in Kainantu. The exceptions were scheduled events or an unforeseen occurrence such as the death of a villager, in which case word spread quickly and within a few hours she would arrive, as much perhaps to be a part of the frenzied activity that surrounds such a rite of passage as to report to work.

Logistically, our work together took two forms. Much of our time was spent with women as they pursued their daily tasks—in their gardens, tending pigs, or sitting in the dooryard netting carrying bags, making bark skirts, or preparing vegetables for an earth oven feast. In an alternative mode, we carried on conversations in a one-room shelter built for the purpose. This gave us a modicum of privacy, although one had to be alert to inquisitive ears that might be glued to a crack in the wall. There was no insulation. Nonetheless, it was a good environment for holding sessions when some structuring was desirable—to limit the number of individuals present, to accumulate knowledge of a personal nature, or to administer projective tests.

Anyan "turned" the two languages, her Tairora and the Tok Pisin we shared, in an exemplary fashion. My expanding knowledge of Tairora was adequate to prompt her if, occasionally, she lost interest or became impatient to the point of encapsulating the translation. It was sometimes difficult for her to understand why I had to ask a woman the same question that had already been answered by several others. Under the circumstances, occasional boredom was understandable.

With the exception of six weeks, when we left the hamlet to

work in a mountain village to the south, she interpreted for me until our exodus from Papua New Guinea in 1955. Neither of us knew if we would see each other again.

But a decade later, in 1963, James and I returned to the highlands to live with the Tairora, half of the time at Abiera, the village where Anyan had grown up. After settling in, I went to Kainantu to renew my acquaintance with Anyan. She was aware of our return, and anticipating that I might again seek her help she and her husband had discussed the possibility of her working with me and the logistics involved. Anyan, with her two toddlers and a new baby, was quite prepared to take up residence at Abiera, a plan her husband had acceded to prior to my contacting her.

Anyan's husband, Robaga, born and raised in a village near the north coast of Papua New Guinea, came into the highlands some time in the early 1940s, as a carrier for Westerners. He found employment and remained in the Kainantu area. When he and Anyan were married he was the cook for a government employee. Throughout most of his working career, Robaga was employed by the Public Health Service serving in a number of capacities, most recently as carpenter.

Our work schedule was flexible and less structured than it had been during the first field trip. I had no work room at Abiera. If privacy was imperative, we gathered in the cook house. Our time was spent informally with the women in their gardens, with their pig herds, or at their houses in the village.

Anyan had sufficient free time that she prepared a small plot on which to grow coffee trees. She was among relatives on whom she could depend for help in clearing the plot, digging holes for the plants, setting out seedlings, and ultimately transplanting them to the garden several hundred feet away. Moreover, she still had claims on land in the village and was able to use a piece of ground that had long lain fallow. Since the plot was grass covered, rather large amounts of labor were necessary to prepare it for horticultural use, but Anyan was fairly successful in manipulating her kin within the bounds of local exchange patterns. All went well and six months after our arrival, shortly before we left Abiera to reside at Batainabura, Anyan gave the customary earth oven feast to repay her helpers.

At Batainabura, a somewhat isolated village at a greater distance from Kainantu than Abiera, one approachable only on foot, our visits to houses and gardens continued. In contrast to grassland Abiera, this area provided the added activity of excursions into the nearby forest. Anyan had time to herself. She lacked the responsibilities of her coffee project at Abiera yet spent no greater amount of time working with me. She produced some crafts, socialized with villagers, and almost daily bathed in the cold river coursing in the valley below.

I know from having explored their way of life with many Tairora women that most of what Anyan says is a good reflection of the general outlines of cultural reality, even if it does not reflect the total range of female behavior. I know too that there are some obvious inconsistencies, some idiosyncracies, and, especially in the myths and stories she recounts, some errors.[2]

Although it is now too late for Anyan to see a dream fulfilled, because she died two decades ago, her biography is completed and her odyssey, pieced together from my field notes, is shared with readers.

This book would not be complete without acknowledgment of my debt to individuals too numerous to list separately. First, my many Tairora friends, especially those living at Haparira, Abiera, and Batainabura at the time of my residence. The expatriates living in the Kainantu area were of great help, including Aubrey and Ancie Schindler, Les and Bess Brady, Harry West, and Bill Brown. I am grateful also to members of the Summer Institute of Linguistics, based at Ukarumpa, especially Alex and Lois Vincent, who have devoted many years to the study and analysis of the Tairora language. Finally, my debt is great to the Ford Foundation and the National Science Foundation as well as James B. Watson, whose grants from those two organizations made possible my ethnographic fieldwork in the highlands of Papua New Guinea.

ANYAN'S STORY

A New Guinea Woman

in Two Worlds

Introduction

"WHEN I WAS BORN MY FATHER HAD FOUR WIVES. MY Mother was number three. She was young and this was her first marriage. Before I was weaned, she died when giving birth to my brother. My father's first wife, who recently lost her baby, was my wet nurse. She is the only one of my father's wives I called 'Mother.' I have always called his other wives by their first names."

Thus begins the life story of Anyan, a Tairora woman who in the course of her life moved from the culture she first learned, one then unknown to the Western world, to an emerging amalgam of Papua New Guinean and Western cultures. As background to her story let us explore briefly the cultural and social world into which she was born.

In an almost idyllic corner of the earth's second largest island live the Tairora, hardy folk well suited to the demands of living in a tropical environment just four degrees south of the Equator. The Tairora are a numerically large group of people occupying a substantial territory that includes a range of topographic features. Although I shall use the term "Tairora" in this monograph, the information was collected among the Northern Tairora. Hidden behind high mountains at an altitude of about 1,600 to 1,700 meters (5,300 to 5,600 feet) above sea level, the region affords a respite from the languishing, energy draining characteristics of a typical tropical paradise. Nights can be very cool, even cold, and the annual range of days from very warm to rather cool. The Tairora profess to having lived in the mountain-ringed, grass-covered valleys, once vast Ice Age lakes, for eons.

During the past half century (roughly 1920 to 1965) many aspects of village life have changed little. With few exceptions the

3

lives of women remain much as they were during Anyan's child-hood and adolescence. Thus it is appropriate to write in the present, changing tense only in those instances where it makes a significant difference for comprehension.

The first Western impulses to be felt by the Tairora, it should be remembered, were tentative. Moreover, at no time in the early decades did these impulses reflect a complete roster of Western culture but rather a highly selective sample: a few miners in search of gold, a few missionaries with their attempts to modify the cleanliness habits and the religious beliefs of the locals, a few individuals engaged in limited commercial enterprises such as trade stores or agricultural pursuits, and a succession of governmental officers of varying rank, whose major tasks were to suppress feuding and establish a modicum of peace among groups of local people accustomed to periodic altercations with one another.[3]

After the Western presence was reestablished in the post-World War II period, with increasing numbers of entrants into the area, its influence intensified. Powerful forces were political (the reimposition of a foreign government) and commercial (vendors providing greater access to Western goods, and producers in need of a labor force).

The effects and extent of these introductions varied in the intensity with which they impinged on the locals. Distance from the government station at Kainantu was an important variable—inhabitants of villages located near the Station being more affected than those farther away. Equally compelling was the mindset of the locals themselves—their attitudes toward newcomers. Upon our arrival in the area, the Tairora were described to us as being the most independent of the four ethnolinguistic groups whose territory impinged on Kainantu. It was reported that they felt little compunction to accede to the blandishments and presumed superiority of the new arrivals. Their greater reserve toward Westerners apparently stemmed from a feeling that they had little to gain from assuming a posture of congeniality and subservience—a posture adopted to some degree by their neighbors.

Tairora subsistence depends on four kinds of activity: horticulture, husbandry, hunting, and collecting. Tairora gardening skills are well developed and organized. Tillage techniques enable them to produce food that sustains their stamina in what is at best an intensely arduous round of activities necessary to provide diet, shelter, clothing, and life itself.

The sweet potato entered the highland's food supply roughly three or four hundred years ago and accounts for a large percentage of the diet. And yams, although produced in relatively small quantities, are of singular importance socially and ceremonially. The time and labor given to growing yams, the creation of a fertile soil of pulverized granules in the elaborately constructed raised beds in which the plants can flourish, and the staking of growing plants, attest to their high value. The winged bean, although less prominent in social life than yams, is accorded similar cultivation, presumably because of its triple supply of food—leaves, beans, and roots—providing a welcome variation in the diet. Two kinds of taro and edible pitpit, bananas, sugar cane, as well as a variety of greens, are among other foods that suggest an ample diet.

Gardens, whether located on the banks of streams, in relatively dry patches, or shaded by a piece of bush, are neatly laid out in squares or rectangles. In preparing them for use, men clear the grass, underbrush, and saplings growing on the plot and they are responsible for erecting the fence around it. The subsequent tilling is performed by women, using long, pointed digging sticks. Planting, tending, harvesting, and transport of the produce to the village are all in the female domain. During Anyan's youth, when enemies could be lurking in the vicinity, men had the additional role of protecting the women toiling in the gardens.

Pigs have long been economically and socially, not merely dietetically, an important food source. The introduction of the sweet potato, a favored pig fodder, permitted a considerable increase in the porcine as well as the human population.

Wild foods, hunted or collected in both grassland and forest, add variety to the diet, although quantities are limited. Included are wild nuts, mushrooms, fowl eggs, insects, birds, eels, and small game. Although most of the small game is eaten immediately, some animals—marsupials especially—are dried and preserved to be used in ritual activities.

Although these foodstuffs still provide a large proportion of the diet, there is an increasing use of rice, canned corned beef, and other foods obtained from trade stores.

When Anyan was a girl, and still today for many Tairora, clothing was scant: a breech cloth for males, a skirt of natural bark strips for females. Girls, almost from birth, wear a small panel of bark strips in front of the pubis. Later, a back panel is added, the sides of the legs and hips remaining visible. After marriage a woman's skirts completely cover the legs, hips, and buttocks. Also worn from then on is a belt to be set aside only during advanced pregnancy or postmenopause. Boys, in contrast to girls, remain naked until age five or six, or even later. Once donning a pubic covering, they have a wider range of styles from which to choose than do girls.

For both males and females, common embellishment consists of woven fiber bands on the upper arm and lower leg as well as plant leaves—dracaena and banana leaves among them—tucked into one's belt. A large net carrying bag worn tumpline fashion by women, a smaller one worn around the neck by a man or slung over his shoulder, in addition to its transport utility also provides some warmth to the wearer's naked torso. The string from which the bags are made is, like the material for men's, women's, and children's clothes made from inner tree bark, often of a kind of ficus. During cold spells, capes made of beaten inner bark of a large forest tree can be worn by those individuals lucky enough to possess one.

Although traditional clothing is still common, with increasing frequency and insofar as it is economically possible, sarongs, trousers, shorts, and shirts are worn by men. A few women wear a sarong and blouse, with more women owning one dress to be worn on special occasions such as the gathering for census taking.

Tairora houses during Anyan's youth were usually circular in configuration, constructed of a pole framework with earthen floor and walls of thatch or bark. These houses tend to be low, primarily for heat retention in the cold highland nights, and the thatch roofs come quite close to the ground to direct rain runoff and prevent splash. Supple and pliant, such houses are admirably suited to go with the flow of the earth as it rumbles beneath them; for earthquakes are a common occurrence. This style of house, although still used, is replaced to varying extent by rectangular structures of pole framework and thatch roof with walls of bamboo planks.

In Anyan's youth, women and children were domiciled in small buildings where they shared space with the pig herd, a partition separating their quarters. In the back half of the house the bare ground served as floor, chair, and bed, and a fire on the hearth was both cooking center and heat generator. Today, men live with their families in this kind of house, but the partition has been removed and the pigs no longer have access. The hearth is centered; in it are roasted sweet potatoes, taro, and yams, while concoctions of greens and other vegetables, with succulent morsels of meat when available, are cooked in bamboo tubes placed directly on the hearth.

Men's houses, now largely a thing of the past, were substantial circular structures. The single room was divided into sections, each containing a hearth and meager furniture—perhaps a three-legged wooden headrest and a mat or two fashioned from pandanus leaves. Spears, bows, arrows, and other accoutrements of the cubicles' occupants were stored in the thatch overhead.

From fifty to a hundred individuals live in each Tairora village, the social arrangements among them being somewhat flexible. Although the lineage of one's mother and mother's brother is important, the system of relationships that permeates one's life is rooted in the dominance of the male line: an individual belongs to the lineage of his father. Sons nominally live with members of that lineage throughout their lifetime, whereas daughters, after marriage, move to live with their husband's kin. Anyan's first residential dislocation was of this kind. Against her desire and against her will, she was betrothed to a man in a village of a different, although related ethnolinguistic group, located closer to the source of western influence, the government station at Kainantu. For Anyan the move to Anona represented a psychological leap of marked proportions.

A man can have more than one wife, all offspring being brothers and sisters to each other. A youngster plays and associates with most children in his extended family or others of the hamlet. These relationships are modified and expanded over time as one's interests and affections change during the growth and maturation process.

Many Tairora of my acquaintance will answer to several names. One name might be bestowed and used by one's paternal kin, a different name by the maternal kin, still another by close child-hood friends. All of the names are known to other Tairora, thus there is no confusion. In these pages I call a person by the same name throughout, including some individuals whose names are changed for the purpose of anonymity.

Marriage is couched largely in terms of family, broadly conceived. An individual marries someone chosen by kinsmen. Bride price and brother-sister exchange are alternative cementing mechanisms. In Anyan's youth, females lived a mode of life that few of them felt compelled to question, let alone resist or rebel against—a system that contained more than a kernel of injustice for them. To some degree it continues.

For women and children the known and familiar world is small. One's counterparts in villages that have no close social ties to one's own are outside the pale. For the society as a whole, men are in charge of maintaining harmony within the smaller social unit, protecting its members from those who would collect raw material for sorcery as, in the past, they protected one from an enemy lurking in the vicinity. During Anyan's youth, feuding was endemic and men preyed on others as they, in turn, were preyed upon. During periods of peace, never permanent, one prepared for the next confrontation with enemies. In both internal and external relations, violence was an integral means of maintaining power. In matters legal and extralegal, physical strength, applied ferociously, was often the final arbiter. With warfare a thing of the past and governmental hegemony established, marked political change has ensued.

A more intangible cultural category, religion broadly conceived as a well-organized, codified whole, is absent among Tairora. All that I attempt here is an itemization of elements, disregarding their positive or negative relationships. There are opposing forces: sun-moon, hot-cold, wet-dry. Supernatural spirits, both good and evil, and other influences that can be categorized under the rubric "souls" are plentiful. Magic and sorcery are powerful and pervasive forces. Females have little or no command of this sort of knowledge although it impinges on them indirectly. It is not an integral part of their perceived world; only through males are Tairora women aware of this as an aspect of the culture. One exception is sorcery, something a few women admit to practicing.

It was against the background of this sort of social climate that Anyan's earliest experiences were cast. When was Anyan born? We cannot with certainty cite a date. Among people with no records, we must rely on circumstantial evidence for vital statistics. On this basis it is realistic to accept that sometime in the 1920s (1923 or 1924?) she was born to Bano and his third wife, Wanama.

Throughout much of Anyan's life the steady progression of cultural change, its ridges and furrows notwithstanding, was a fact of life. Even as she was becoming enculturated, changes that were unseen by the locals—changes that may have been unforeseeable— were being put in place.

The changes were so far-reaching that by the end of the period documented by this life history, the people of the Papua New Guinea highlands had moved from their precolonial status to one in which they became participants in the Western electoral process. They were on the verge of occupying a place of political independence in the world.

This, then, must serve as a very encapsulated background for Anyan's story. The more detailed, definitive discussion of Northern Tairora culture is found in *Tairora Culture: Contingency and Pragmatism* by James B. Watson, published in 1983 by the University of Washington Press.

All Play, No Work

WHEN I WAS BORN MY FATHER HAD FOUR WIVES. MY Mother was number three. She was young and this was her first marriage. Before I was weaned, she died when giving birth to my brother. My father's first wife, who recently lost her baby, was my wet nurse. She is the only one of my father's wives I called "Mother." I have always called his other wives by their first names.

Not long after I was weaned I was sent to live with my mother's brother in another village. At that time my father moved over the mountain to live near his large pig herd, and from then on I seldom saw any of that group. I grew up thinking my maternal uncle was my father. I called him Father. I thought his first wife was my Mother. It was not until many, many years later that I learned who my true father and mother were. I do not remember my real mother or anything from that early time.

My biological father was a powerful leader of the tribe. He was a Big Man. In his lifetime he had five wives, one of whom he beat to death after seeing her in adulterous passion with another man. Quite by accident he fatally wounded one of his own lovers.

My maternal uncle, Mando, had five wives in his lifetime but only two when I went to live with them. His first wife, Taramao, brought me up. She had had a baby shortly before I came to live with them, but the baby died so I was like her only child at the time. Tabare, the second wife, was then childless. These two women were Mando's wives when I came to live with them. I thought Taramao was my real mother. I also called Tabare "Mother," because she too was my father's wife, but I didn't feel close to her and I didn't like her much nor did I mind her well. She would often get angry with me because I favored Taramao. "You should treat me better because I am your Mother too, I am your Father's wife," she would say to me. It is true that both she and Taramao looked after me, but I liked Taramao better and minded her best of all. I thought she was my real Mother.

Mando's two wives shared a house and they got along fairly well with one another. If co-wives did not get along a man had to build a house for each of them, sometimes in different sections of the village, sometimes in different villages. In the time I am talking of, Mando had only one house for his two wives and they got along fairly well together. But sometimes they would fight. They would yell and shout at each other and I remember a few times when they hit each other with sticks. But they both looked after me and I helped both of them when I was old enough.

In those days men did not sleep in the same house as their wives but at one of the men's houses, which were at some distance from the women's houses. The women's houses were separated from the men's by a large strip of ground. Mando slept in one of the men's houses with his close male relatives. All of his possessions, his bows and arrows, net bags, bamboo flutes, were kept at the men's house—a house into which only men and initiated boys could go.

Every day his wives would cook food and send it to Mando at the men's house, for the men did not do much cooking there. Some-times I would take the food to him. There was a hedge around the large house and I could not go beyond it. I would go to the open-ing in the hedge and call out, "Mando, here is your food. Come and get it." Sometimes he would take it right away, sometimes he would send a boy for it, and other times I would just leave the food there and he would fetch it later. This was not a good thing though, for if it was left very long, pigs might eat it, or worse, an enemy might take some of it to use in sorcery. It was best if the food was taken into the men's house right away, but because I was a girl I could not go beyond the hedge.

So I lived with Mando and his wives. After several years Tabare had a baby boy called Haru. He was quite a bit younger than me. Tabare did not take very good care of him even when he was a tiny baby. When she went to the garden to work she left him in the village in my care. When he got hungry he cried and cried and I would take him to the garden so Tabare could nurse him. As soon as he was satisfied she would give him back to me. So I took care of Haru a lot of the time when he was a baby and a little boy. He and I had the same Father, although different mothers, so according to the traditions of our people, we were considered brother and sister. I was his big sister. He was my little brother.

Ika was also my brother, although we did not have the same biological father or mother. His father was the elder brother of my father, so that made Ika and me brother and sister. Ika was younger than me but older than Haru. Because I was the eldest I had to care for both boys and we were often together. Sometimes I would get cross with them but I don't remember ever hitting them. One time when I became angry with Ika, though, I burned his arm. I had made a fire on the hearth; the wood was damp and I had to work hard on it. Just when the fire was going fairly well, Ika scattered the wood all around and the fire went out. This made me very angry, so I took a red hot stick and burned his arm with it. You can still see the scar. His mother was not cross with me for doing it; she said that he had been misbehaving and deserved punishment.

Although Mando was my real father, I had other fathers too. All of Mando's brothers were my fathers. They treated me very well. Mando was the only one who punished me. He didn't punish me often, but sometimes he would hit me with a stick if I did something that angered him. Sometimes when he did this I would get so frightened that I would shit and piss right there. Usually it went on the ground, but once or twice it got on his hand. I guess that shows that Mando was considered my true father. He really was my mother's brother, and it is bad for a child to soil a maternal uncle—very, very bad. But he didn't mind because he thought of himself as my father. He did not hit me often but when he did I was so frightened that I couldn't help shitting or pissing. Children often did this when they were hit with sticks.

My other fathers never hit me, even when they were angry. I remember one time when Beja told me to go to a stream and fetch water in a bamboo tube. It was raining hard outside and I didn't want to go that far. So I went just part way and got some water from along the path. When I returned he knew I had deceived him and he was angry. He poured all the water on my head and made me go back for more, but he did not hit me. He was my father because he was my father's brother.

We believe that it is good to have many brothers. Then children have many fathers, because all their real father's brothers are their fathers too. We have many stories about how important brothers are. Once upon a time the two wives of a man fought a lot, and it was the same wife who always started the fights. One day she sharpened the leg bone of a pig, and the next time there was a fight she shoved it into the back of her co-wife's neck. The woman wasn't punished for this. She had many, many relatives. She had a lot of brothers, and the other co-wife didn't have many brothers. So the woman who cut the other one was not punished. Her parents had many children and she was the only girl, so she had a lot of brothers to protect her. Otherwise she would have been punished for doing this. There is a song about this woman. Her name is Ona.

Brothers not only protected their sisters but they helped and protected each other. Here is another story. Some young boys, three brothers, shot some fish with their bows and arrows. They put the fish on a rock to dry in the sun. A man who lived in a large house nearby, a big man who was blind in one eye, waited in the house. The three brothers came near the house. Then two of them left. The two who left thought the other brother would follow them, but he got caught in a rainstorm. He tried to go inside the man's house but he couldn't find a door, so he climbed on top of the house and came down the center pole. He looked around. He saw the man and he saw cassowaries, opossums, and other animals the man had trapped. The man got a clay jar full of food that had been cooked the day before. The boy ate one piece and the blind man ate one piece. Then the boy ate something else and the man ate something else. Finally they ate all the food in the clay jar. Then they ate the food in another jar. The boy ate some and the blind man ate some. They ate and ate. They ate all the food that was in the clay jars.

Then the man took hold of the boy's wrist. He said, "Who is this? Is it my grandson?" The boy said, "I came with two other boys who have run away, but I stayed." The man said, "You go get some water and cook the animals. We can cook them together. Bring water. Get the fire ready." While the boy was working the man took a big stick. He hit the boy in the back of the neck and killed him. Then the man cut up the animals, he cut up the boy, and he mixed them all together. He had enough food to fill ten clay jars. The man cooked the food and then put it away. He planned to eat it in the morning.

By this time the boy's two brothers were looking for him. They came to the rock where they had left the dried fish. They said, "This is the rock. We caught fish and we left them here to dry. They are still here. Where is our brother?" The two brothers looked and looked for the third boy. They went inside the house but they could not find him. They saw the food that had not been eaten. They tasted some and they knew there was human flesh. They knew it was their brother. They put a jar of food outside the house. Then they stood holding their bows and arrows. When the man came out of the house to get the food, the two boys shot him. Then they put the dead man in the house and they set fire to it. The man and the house burned up. The two brothers went home quickly. They showed the food to their father and mother and to their family. They all knew it was their brother. Then they ate the food.

It is especially important for a man's family to treat his wife's brother with respect because he will be mother's brother to the man's children. He will be important to them in many ways. Although he belongs to a different lineage, he is important. The next story tells why the Tairora and Kamano have long been enemies.

A Tairora woman married a Kamano man and went to live in his village, Twimpinka. After a while she had a baby boy. He grew and grew. When it was time for him to be initiated she went back to her village and told her brother to come. He came and stayed in the men's house. The woman thought the Kamano were feeding her brother but they did not feed him. They did not give him sugar cane or any other food. All of the people in the village ate but they did not give food to the boy's maternal uncle. The man became very hungry. The people did not look after him and bring him food. He was maternal kin of one of them but they did not treat him right. They were not good to him.

One night there was a big storm. The man took his sister and her son back to Tairora country. Then he got all dressed up. He put on dracaena leaves and other plant decorations. With these on he could walk safely in the storm. The lightning would not harm him. Then he went back to Twimpinka. He surprised the men in the men's house and killed all of them. Since that time the Kamano and Tairora have not been friends.

As I have told you, when I was a little girl, Mando was good to me. My mother died and I might have died too if Mando hadn't looked after me. He gave me food and clothes, took me to his house, and took good care of me. My real father didn't want to keep me after my mother died.

So when I was a young girl I lived in a village and played mostly with children nearby, but sometimes, later on, we would play with children in other villages. The villages then were different from what they are now. They were smaller and the men lived at the men's house and not with their wives as most of them do now. They would build separate houses for their wives and children. The women's houses were always in a part of the village away from the men's house. Not only did women and children live in these houses but they shared them with their pigs. The small round houses were divided into two rooms connected by a door at one side of the partition between them. People lived, ate, and slept in the back room. The front room was for the pigs. There were two doors at the front of the house—a large doorway through which people passed, although grown-ups had to stoop a bit, and a very small one next to it through which the pigs could come and go when the larger door was closed. The large door was different from the ones we have now. It was a vertical opening that was framed by double upright posts. During the day if we were away from the house, and at nighttime, we put the flat, planklike slats between the posts.

Another difference from today was the growth of grass within the village. We did not clear it away to have only bare ground around the houses as we do now—a practice forced on us by the government. The grass grew tall around the houses and we would walk through it and sit on it. The pigs would lie on it and walk through it too. Some grass around the houses became flattened because we sat and walked on it so much, but it was never cleared away as it is today. A few older people still keep a patch of grass near the house so they can sit on it because it feels good. But most of us are becoming used to sitting on the bare earth, something we didn't have to do when I was growing up.

Because I had to take care of them, Ika and Haru and I played together a great deal when we were small children. There is still a big tree from which we used to swing. We made toys by bending pieces of coarse grass to make figures of various kinds—houses, adzes, people, things like that. We also made whistles out of bent grass stems by holding them between our thumbs and blowing on them. We learned how to make string figures (cat's cradles) too, not only the simple ones but those for which we used our toes as well as our hands. Most string figures we made by ourselves, but there are some that two people can do together. Girls are usually better at string figures than boys, but we all made them when we were young.

We played many games in the tall grass. There was one woman who was crazy. Although she lived to be an old woman, she always behaved like a child. She liked to play with children and some-times we would play with her. We would grab her arms and pull her through the long grass. Sometimes we formed two lines, made her run between them, and as she passed we kicked her. We would do this with each other too; a group of girls playing together could play this game.

One thing that all children like to do is steal food. Not only do they have fun taking it but they like to eat what they get. Most often they take bananas or sugar cane but also other things. I did not steal much from gardens but I remember a few times when I did. Once, when I was about seven years old, three girl friends and I were walking near Kuboo's garden. It was a good garden—large, with lots of greens and sweet potatoes. I said, "Let's steal some of the food and take it with us." They agreed and we all put food in our net bags and started on our way. Kuboo saw us leaving the garden and suspected that we had stolen some food. She yelled at us, scolded us, and told us to come back. But we didn't. We ran. We knew she couldn't catch us and we knew that later on she might scold us again but she wouldn't do anything else to us.

Another time, several years later, I was walking by a garden that belonged to an old woman. It was during the rainy season. The greens were fresh and the sweet potatoes were big and just ready to eat. They were very good ones. I stole some of each, took them home, cooked them, and ate them all up at once.

As I passed by a large garden one night when we kids were hunting rats, I decided to steal some food. I wasn't hungry, but there was a lot of food and I decided to take some. I dug up some sweet potatoes, picked some edible pitpit and greens, and then began to leave. I discovered that I had picked too much to put in my small net bag, so I took what I could and hid the rest in the tall grass. The next day I sneaked back and got that too. No one had found it.

There were four girls I used to go around with a great deal: Teba, Kainoba, Apam, and Amay. Amay and I were born about the same time and our mothers said that we would be special friends, that we should play together, help one another, and always consider each other best friends. This is one of our customs. The mothers of two girls who are born at the same time will say to each other, "Our girls were born together, they should become special friends and remain best friends forever. That should happen." The girls, then, are very close for a long while, sometimes throughout life. They help one another and if they live in the same village after they are married they continue this close friendship for life. Our mothers made Amay and me special friends. But other girls were good friends of mine too and actually I played with Teba and Apam more than with Amay, although she and I knew that our mothers had made us special friends.

One of the things we girls did was hunt rats on moonlit nights. Most children liked to do this, and on a moonlit night plenty of kids would go rat hunting and you could hear them yelling and shouting with joy as they tried to find the rats. It was a lot of fun. One time when Teba and Kainoba and I were hunting rats we had good luck. Teba was always quite good at catching rats. She was quick and she would catch one with her hands and pin it down to the ground so it couldn't get away. When we caught rats we would break their legs so they couldn't run. Just snap their legs with our fingers. We didn't want to share the rats with other children, as we should have done, so we didn't tell the others how many rats we caught. We would hide them in certain places and later go back and get them when no one knew about it. That way we would have a lot more rats to eat then if we told the truth.

When I was young, older people would hunt rats too. As a rule they would not eat the rats but would give them to us children. After the rats were caught, we would put them on a fire which had burned down, singe off the hair, and roast them. We turned them from time to time by twisting their tails. We roasted them slowly so they would not pop open and their guts spill out on the ground. We wanted to have every bit, not lose any of the juices. After they were roasted the whole rat could be eaten—all parts of it.

We did not hunt them only on moonlight nights. Another good time for hunting was when the field grass was being burned. If someone was making a new garden and wanted to burn the grass off before he started to prepare the ground, or if someone had an old pile of dry grass and brush that he had cleared from a garden plot and that he wanted to burn, everyone would stand around waiting for the rats to run out of the fire. There were always a lot of rats in the long grass, and when the grass burned they would run out and we would catch them. Sometimes too we would find the houses of rats and there would be little rats and we would get them and eat them too. They were especially good, very tender and sweet. Or if someone tore down an old house we would wait nearby to catch the rats that were living in the thatch. Now, most of us no longer eat rats because the White man has told us that it is a bad thing. But children still eat them and like them and old people do too.

We often stayed fairly close to the village when we were young but sometimes we wandered quite far away. One time Apam went to Ontenu with her father and mother to fetch firewood. Teba, Kainoba, and I were to follow them later and help bring the wood back to the village. We got caught in a big rainstorm near the Ramu River and we didn't want to go on. We thought we would spend the night in a pig house near the river. We were alone and had no grown-up person, no big man with us for safety. We knew that a woman who had died recently was buried nearby and we were very frightened. We were very frightened because we knew that the spirit of such a strong young woman as she had been would have a very powerful ghost. But we went in the house, built a fire, cooked some food and ate it. We were alone and we were very afraid that something would get us. So we pretended that there were some men with us. We made believe that we were men smoking bamboo pipes and we made the noises they would make. You have heard the whooshing sounds they make with their bamboo smoking tubes. We talked in deep voices and talked about things men would talk about—joking and laughing too.

Another thing we were afraid of was the skull man. Would he come after us? We didn't know. One of our stories says he was killed long ago. But people are still afraid that he might come again. Once some men and women from a village near Bontaa were going to go to Aiyura for a dance. They got all dressed up in their finery. One woman and her child had sores all over their bodies. They did not go. They stayed home. After the others left they gathered greens, then they cooked them and ate them.

When they finished eating they wanted to sleep. The skull man came and found them. There were loud noises by the house. The woman and her child went out to look. They saw the skull man and they talked with him. They were frightened. Then they saw a rat. They talked to the rat. They said, "Your house is up on the mountain. You make a hole in the ground. We want to go inside and fool people." This is the way they talked. The rat left to make a hole. He dug and dug. Then he came back and spoke to the two. "It is all right now for you two to come. You can come up to my house now." This is what he said. The woman put the child in her net bag.

She went inside the hole. The two went in the hole. They walked and walked and walked. They came to an open place. They made a fire. They saw the skull man. He spoke. The woman cried now. The skull man said, "I am very sorry. I won't hurt you."

The two walked again. Later they stopped and built a fire. Then the skull man came. The woman and child saw it and started to walk again. When they were away from him they built a fire. The skull man saw it. He said, "You two are trying to fool me. Where have you gone now?"

The skull man kept following them. He saw the two and wanted to get beside them. Finally, the woman and child arrived where all the men and women were having the dance. The two sat down and people asked them why they had come. They said someone had been following them. "Who has been following you?" They told them that the skull man had been following them.

Then all the men got their bows and arrows. They sang a song. They shot at the skull man. He was trying to get at the woman and child. All the men shot at it and it exploded. Now they say that they killed the skull man in this area. And the pigs ate it. They killed it completely. After the dance was over all the people went back to their village. So that night as we girls sat alone around that fire, we worried that something might get us. We were still frightened of the skull man. But finally we went to sleep.

At dawn we got up and went out to get some worms so we could fish in the river. We got a lot of fish in the little stream just this side of the Ramu. Bajnti came along in a while and we gave him some fish. He gave us some yams so we didn't have to steal any from the gardens there. It would have been easy because none of the people were in their gardens.

Then Bajnti offered to help us find the way to Ontenu. He told us not to be afraid of any enemies that might be lurking on the way there. "It is true that an enemy can hit you and even kill you, but you should try not to be frightened and walk right along," he told us.

After a while we came to the Ramu River itself, but the water was high from all the rain and we could not cross it so we slept in a house that was nearby. Bajnti stayed with us. The next day we crossed the river and went through Kamano territory to Ontenu. Later we came home.

When we children misbehaved we were told stories of bad spirits who would harm us or of people who would work sorcery upon us. I was told that Taribaj would make sorcery against me if I didn't behave. My parents would show me some tabooed food that was like the kind that he gave people to poison them. I was told never to eat it but to throw it away. We were also told never to take food from people we didn't know or people who weren't relatives of ours.

One time when I was about eight years old, Matabeba gave me some roasted grubs. He had a lot of them and he gave me some. I took them and as I continued walking along the path I ate some of them. I soon met Norihu, who asked to see the grubs so I showed them to him. He wanted to keep half and I agreed. I continued walking and a bit further on I met Beja. He ate some of the grubs but at the same time he told me that I shouldn't take things from people who were not in my family. That that wasn't a good way to behave. He said, "If you take food from people you don't know well you can't go to the place of our ancestors." Then he threatened to hit me with a stick, but he didn't to it. Just threatened. That time he also said that I shouldn't walk around alone so much. I should stay nearer the village when I wasn't with other children. After that I didn't walk around on the footpaths as much as I had before. I was frightened to do it.

He told me a story about something that happened to a girl a long time ago. It was one time when young boys were going to be initiated. Early in the morning of the big feast a young girl went to the garden to dig sweet potatoes. When she got to the garden she heard a snake calling to her. She did not see the snake but the snake kept calling her name. She looked and looked for it, but she couldn't find it.

Back in the village the men and women were getting things ready for the earth oven feast. At the garden the girl kept looking for the snake. Since snakes live in mature bamboos, she broke one bamboo after another. She broke all but one. Only one large bamboo remained and a man came out of it. He was a snake-man. The girl followed him to the forest. She did not go back to the village. The people were busy and did not look for her. They just forgot her. After a while she had a child, and she and the baby stayed in the forest with the snake-man. Now all the men still sing about this woman when they are in the men's house during the boys' initiation.

At least twice when I was young I was very sick. The first time I was at Abiera. One day Taramao left me alone in the house when she went to the garden to get food. While she was gone, one of Bano's wives, Aruo, with her sisters and brothers, came to see me. They brought a pig head and jaw with the tongue and part of the neck still on it. They told me it was for me. They said they would leave it on the table and someone could cook it for me. Aruo then took me to the river and gave me a bath, wiping me afterward with several kinds of grass and leaves—kinds we used before we had towels. Then they carried me back to Mando's house and left for their home, which was in another village.

When Taramao came back I told her that the pig head was there to be cooked. She said, "There is no pig here. None at all." I said, "Oh, yes. It's there on the table." Then I told her about the people bringing it to me. I described the head, tongue, jaw, and neck of the pig. She said, "You're crazy. There is no pig here." Long afterward, when I had been well for quite a while, I saw Aruo one day and asked her if she had visited me. She said, "Oh, no. I would be afraid to do that. You were living in an enemy village then. I would be afraid to come and see you. No, I didn't bring you any pig."

Then I knew that it was my sickness that caused this. It wasn't a real dream, but was like a dream. During this sickness someone was trying to make me die. The spirit offered me the pig jaw to eat to make me die. If a person is sick and the spirit of another person comes and gives him food, if the sick one eats it right away he will die. He tells the spirit he will eat it later. Tells him to put it on the table. Then the sick person will not die. I told the spirit to put the jaw on the table and I would eat it later.

Another time when I was very sick at Ihua's house I would see a big pool of water. The water in the pool was not smooth. There were big waves on it. I saw this several times. I also felt big earthquakes at this time. I was very ill and my relatives did not think I would get well. Ihua did not take much care of me then. She did not clean up my shit and piss. She left me alone a lot of the time, and when she was gone these things would happen. At one point I began to feel better but then I got sick again. I was very sick. The spirit really had hold of me and didn't want to let go. Mando went to another village and got a pig. He took it back to Abiera, cooked part of it in a bamboo tube and gave some of it to me to eat. I was close to dying. He shut the door and left me in the house. They decided to have an earth oven feast and all my relatives came, all of my brothers and sisters and other relatives. Mando made cuts by my ribs with a shiny black stone. This was to let the bad blood out so I would get well. During this illness, I shook a great deal and I was very, very hot. I was thirsty too. I couldn't talk or make much sense. I couldn't get up to go out to pee. I was like a baby. Many people came to see me, all of my relatives. I guess they thought I was going to die.

After I had been bled, my aunt carried me down to the stream to wash me. I was about six years old I think. She washed me with a wildflower. Then she wrapped me in a bark blanket and took me back to the house. She thought that I was dying. I was washed at the stream several times, and each time a different plant was used. Then I was taken back to the house and left alone. I would cry. A spirit would come and talk to me. I saw it. I didn't like it. I knew it meant nothing good for me. But I was strong. I would look directly at the spirit and I did not die. After a while it let me alone, I got better, and soon I was able to get up and walk around. I was well again.

I was very young at this time. Although I don't know to this day whose spirit made me sick, it was my own mother's spirit who took me to the river and washed me. It really didn't happen, I guess. I just thought it did.

In the early days girls and boys had holes made in their noses and ears. When I was quite young, six or seven years old perhaps, the hole was made between my nostrils. This hole is made at a certain time of the year: the time of shooting pigs, the time of the big sun, the time when there is no rain, the time when there is not a lot of food. It is always done at this time of year. It was done to eight of us girls at the same time.

One day we all gathered in the village. There were other people there too, both men and women. We girls were frightened because we really did not know what was going to happen to us. We had heard rumors, but we didn't know for sure. The men were doing a lot of walking around and talking with one another. After a while, the men began speaking to us girls as we sat around the fire. They told us that a hole would be made in our noses, between the nostrils. As we sat by the fire the men told us to put our thumb and forefinger right by the hot coals, to get them as hot as we could stand, then to place them, one finger on either side of the nasal septum. The men told us to do this many times to heat up the skin, to make it soft and thus easier to pierce. They said it wouldn't hurt as much if we did.

After we had done this for a while one man got behind each of us girls. In my case it was Mando who was going to make the hole. He stood behind me and put his left hand on the left side of my face. In his right hand was a piece of bone from the leg of a pig which he had sharpened to a fairly fine point with a stone tool. He put the point against my septum and jabbed it in to make a hole in the skin. After he had done this, he repeatedly pushed the bone into the septum, making it deeper and deeper each time. He pushed the bone in, pulled it out, pushed it in, pulled it out, again and again. He held my head very tight so it would not turn away from him as he operated.

After a while he stood in front of me, put his left hand on the right side of my head, and repeated the operation from the other side of my nose. He pushed and pulled and sometimes he would twist the bone tool in the hole, which was small at first but kept getting larger. He wanted to make a good hole that would last forever.

This hurt a great deal, and although we were supposed to pretend that it didn't, we could not help crying out from time to time. It hurt some of us more than others, and some of the girls cried a great deal and tried to get away. But most of us were good and tried to hold still because we knew that it was a custom of our people to do this. It was necessary if we were to grow up to be good strong women. After Mando had made a good hole he removed the bone tool. There was not much blood in this operation. That part of the nose does not have much blood.

After he was finished Mando put a piece of reed in the hole so it would remain open. The reed had to be replaced every so often and several pieces were used before the hole completely healed. I don't remember how many reeds were used. After healing was complete I didn't have to keep anything in the hole, although we often put a piece of reed or grass stem in it. On special occasions I would wear a long piece of white stone in the hole. The white stone was one that Mando shaped and gave to me.

When the holes had been made in all of our noses there was a big feast. The women filled the earth oven in the morning and by the time the operation was over the food was ready. Besides the food a lot of gifts were given to our maternal relatives—bark cloth, bark blankets, bows and arrows, pigs, and many other things. Making this hole in a girl's or boy's nose was very important when I was young. It was absolutely necessary and if a child died before the hole was made it would be made in the corpse. The hole in the septum was the first one made in my nose. The other hole was made several years later when I was about ten years old.

The holes in my ears were made when I was a baby. I don't know just when they were made but I was very tiny. We still do it to babies. Usually a mother sharpens a piece of bamboo and with this she makes a hole in each earlobe of her child. She then tears a piece of bark string from one of the skirts she is wearing and puts it through the hole as if she were threading a needle. The string stays there until the hole is healed. From time to time she moves the string, pulling it back and forth, to ensure that the hole does not close. When I was older I wore different things in these ear holes— a piece of coconut husk was the most common, but sometimes I put straw or small reeds in.

The other hole in my nose, the one that goes through the tip, this small hole that you see, was done one time after our men came back from a fight. An enemy had been killed. The men came back and told us all about it, about how it happened, about all of the things that happened during the fight. At that time holes were made in the tips of our noses. There were five or six of us girls and we were all about the same age. However, sometimes girls don't have this hole made in their nose until they are quite old. The rules about this are not as strict as about the other hole in our nose.

This hole in my nose was made by my cousin, but any woman can do it. Your mother or your aunt could do it. It is made with a very fine piece of bamboo. The hole is made from the outside of the nose into the nostril. It is usually made in the right nostril. Mine was. There isn't much blood in this hole piercing—I don't think I bled at all—but there is a lot of pain. It hurt me a great deal. After the hole had healed Mando gave me a bone from the wing of a fruit bat to wear in it. All women used to wear these but only a few do now, although many of us still have the hole in our nose and we have kept the curved bones even though we don't wear them.

The big hole in my nose was made first and the small one later on. But it doesn't matter which one is made first. It all depends on when they want to do it to you. A girl does not have anything to say about it. It is something that should be done, and our fathers and maternal relatives know the proper time.

When I told you about Beja telling me not to walk around on the roads so much I should have told you about some things that used to happen a long time ago, when we were still warlike people, the time when there was always the possibility of fighting. In those days we had friends and we had enemies. Much of the time there was no fighting but we could never be sure that our enemies weren't lurking nearby, ready to attack us.

My people have been fighters for a long time and there was always the chance that fighting would break out. In those days it was not considered safe for people to walk very far from the village and certainly not alone. At times when we were wary of a certain enemy it was not safe for people to work alone in their gardens. A man would go to the garden with his wife to be on guard, so he could shoot an enemy if one appeared. A woman would never go out alone on the footpaths; her husband would be with her to protect her.

In those times too, everyone lived inside the village and the villages were palisaded. There was only one door—a door that was guarded most of the time. It was not wise to have a house a long way from the village. I remember one time when two men built a house away from the village so they could catch rats more easily. It was a small round house made of woven bamboo and reeds, about twelve feet in diameter. These two men would go out there and hunt rats and sometimes they would stay there all night. People told them they shouldn't do this because the enemy might get them. They were not afraid and didn't listen to what people told them. They said, "There are no enemies around now. Everyone is our friend. We want to catch a lot of rats and we are not afraid to stay there."

One night they hunted rats. When they were finished they went inside the house. They built a fire and were going to eat and then sleep. Soon a lot of men came from Arogara, quietly sneaking up on the two men. The Arogaras shot arrows into the house. One man was killed. The other was wounded in the leg and in the chest. They caught him and tied him to the center post of the house. The house was then set afire and the enemy fled. Somehow the wounded man freed himself, jumped clear of the fire, and survived. I don't know how he did it but he did. He returned to the village and was ill for a long time but finally got well.

There was always the possibility that a few or even one enemy might attack people while they were away from the village. They would sneak up on them and shoot at them. Our men did that to our enemies too. But in a real fight, many people participated. Sometimes people from several villages would join to attack a particular enemy village. If our men went quite far away they would always leave some men in the village to protect the women and children. Some men didn't like to fight and they would stay to protect the others. They were called "cold" men. The men who liked to fight and were the great fighters were called "hot" men. If the fighting was close to our village or if the enemy came here to attack us, everyone would leave the village and go up on the mountain until the fighting was over.

Men were always prepared to fight. They kept their bows, arrows, and shields in the men's house. Each man stored his weapons in the thatch over the spot where he slept. Some men kept some of their gear in their wives' houses too. I remember one time our men were going to fight the enemy. They didn't tell us children what was going to happen. There was a big feast. The men stayed together and the women didn't go to eat with them, but some of us young girls went. I didn't know it then but the men thought that if they didn't have this feast the enemy would shoot them and kill them. Neither did we know that the men bled their noses before they went to fight.

After the men had eaten, they slept and then at dawn they arose and decorated themselves with red and black "paint" and went to the place they were going to fight. The first time a man fought he would also smear clay on his body but usually he didn't do this in future fights—just used charcoal paint. When they got near the enemy village they hid in the woods or tall grass and as the men came out they shot them, one by one. But the first men who were attacked would cry out to the other people, and the rest of the men would come out ready to shoot our men.

When the shooting had gone on a while our men would go where their wives were waiting and cooking food for them. Some women would usually go with their husbands on these big fights.

A man would leave one or two wives at home, but the others went with him. He would choose who could go. The women carried extra bows and arrows and food, and they did the cooking. They would stay away from where the actual fighting took place. I don't know if it is true but I have heard that some women would shoot too. Usually, however, women don't know how to shoot bows and arrows. That is something for men. Arat says that her mother used to shoot at the enemy and that she killed some of them. Arat, herself, didn't learn to shoot. I don't know if what she says about her mother is really true. She is such a liar. The fighting might go on for several days and then stop for a while.

The women who went to fight usually dressed up like the men. The men painted themselves with black and red paint and the women did too. They painted their faces black with charcoal as the men did. The women also put braided bark belts around their waists, over one shoulder and under the other arm. After the fighting was finished they would return to the village, take the belt off, and burn it. They also washed off the charcoal.

If a man was killed during these fights he was brought back to the village. If necessary, women would carry him. If a man died everyone would come to mourn for him after he was brought back. The men would shoot arrows into a special tree and people would chew the bark of this tree. If an enemy man was killed, a lot of arrows would be shot into him after he was dead. This happened to some of our men too. I remember when they brought Ereo back. His body was covered with blood. He had been killed in a fight. There was a big feast afterward. Later the men went to fight the same enemy and they killed two of their men.

A man killed in war was placed on a rack to rot. Later his bones were buried or put in a cave. After a while the dead man's brothers would fight the same enemy. When one of the enemy was killed the man who had killed him would go to the bones of the first man and tell him that it was all right now that he had killed one of the enemy. The spirit of the dead man would not bother any of us anymore.

At Barabuna they did something that we didn't do. When a man was killed while fighting they would dig a hole and then put arrows in the hole, standing them up so the tips pointed straight up. Then they would lay the body on these arrow points. There were enough arrows to hold up the body. As it rotted, parts of the body would drop into the hole. After all of it had fallen, it was covered up. We didn't do that, but we always heard that they did it at Barabuna.

Sometimes no one was killed in a fight but maybe just the houses were burned or the gardens ruined. The attackers would steal all the food from the gardens after the people had run away. Then they couldn't come back to live there for a while. This would happen to different people. Their village would be burned and their gardens ruined and they would have to go somewhere else and live for a while. They would have to live with friends or relatives. That was the way it was when I was a little girl.

We have many stories about how people destroyed villages. One of them is about a man who pretended he was dead. He killed a bug and he put it to his nose to smell it. He spoke. He made a place to lie down and he lay down. He put a lot of arrows in a new net bag and put them close to the place where he was lying. He said, "You have heard that I am going to die. That I am almost dead." He said this and then he pretended to die. He held his arms and legs stiff. Even if a fly came on him, on his leg or on his nose, he did not move. He did not shoo the fly away, but let it stay there. Everyone came to see him. They came to feel his skin. To be sorry for him. To wail and cry for him. Then when they were all there he jumped up. He grabbed his bow and arrows. He shot all of them. He killed them all. Then he went to another village and did the same thing to the people there. He did this in many places. He destroyed many villages.

We have a story, too, about how one man could start a new village, how he could begin new lineages. There was once a Tairora man who had very little food. He knew about stones for earth ovens. He knew about heating the stones. He knew how to cook food. But he didn't have much food to cook. This man built several houses. He put a fence around them. But he still had almost no food. He built fires in all of the houses. There was only smoke, He went to the men's house and called out in a loud voice, "Go get pandanus nuts. Kill a lot of animals. Bring them to me here at the men's house." He called in a deep voice. He did this at all the houses. He went from one house to another saying to bring pandanus nuts and animals.

A man and his daughter from another village came by. They saw the smoke coming from all the houses. They heard the man shouting from his house to bring pandanus nuts and animals. They thought, "There are a lot of people here at this village." They said, "We want to live with you." The man replied, "All right. You two can stay here. Get some pandanus mats and make a bed. I'll get food for you from the women's houses." He found some food, cooked it, and gave it to the man and his daughter. Then he said, "You two stay here. I'll go get some firewood for you."

He got wood from each of the houses. All the time he was talking. He brought the firewood. They all slept. Morning came. The first man kindled a fire and then went outside. He said, "You two stay here. I'll go get more food, firewood, and stones. We will have an earth oven feast. You two can eat. Then, afterward you can go. Now I will go get food from all the women and make an earth oven." Then he called out, "The stones are hot, bring the food." The two guests thought he was calling out to real people. The man got water and poured it on the stones. He killed a pig. "Bring a lot of food," he shouted.

The girl watched this man. She thought there were a lot of people there but there weren't. She said, "Papa, I want to stay here forever. I do not want to leave when you do." The father said, "All right. You stay here." The father took some food and he left. The girl stayed. Later she had a baby. Then she had another child. She had many children.

One day a bird came and shit on the ground. From this yam plants grew. The people gave it a name. Then another plant came up. They named it. Then another and another came up. Finally, sweet potatoes grew. Now there was all kinds of food.

Then it was time for the first child to marry. Then another child married. Then another. After all of these had children they gave line names to the lineages that were being made. After that, as children grew up they kept their line names.

We also have a story about how the first Tairora started—a story about how everything came up for the first time. There were two brothers who lived over near Kamungera. The older brother was collecting pandanus nuts and he told his younger brother to put them out to dry as he brought them in. The older brother went to the woods to get more nuts.

While he was gone the younger brother ate some of the nuts. When the older brother came back he did not notice that the younger brother had eaten the nuts. He went back to the forest to get more nuts. While he was gone the younger brother ate some more nuts. When the older brother came back this time he saw the holes in the husks and asked, "Where are the nuts?" The younger brother said, "I don't know, I didn't see them. Maybe some children ate them. I haven't seen them. I didn't eat them." This is what the younger brother told the older brother. The older brother said, "You are not telling the truth. You ate them. You are lying to me." The two brothers had a big fight and the older brother won. The younger brother was beaten badly. His clothes were scattered all around. His teeth went in one direction, his body in another.

But he did not die. He left. He went down near Barabuna. He found good land. He grew better things than where he had been before. Then two women from the coast came into the area. They were following fish in the water. The younger brother married both of these women. The older brother still had no wife. The two brothers had separated. The women made good gardens for the younger brother.

The older brother went to visit them. He was very skinny. His eyes were glassy. He had no food. The younger brother was in the forest when the older brother came. The wives of younger brother went into the forest to tell him that older brother had come.

Younger brother came back in the form of a pig. He attacked older brother and threw him up in a tree. Then he went back to the forest. After a while he came back to the house as a man. He welcomed his older brother and told him to eat a lot of food. The older brother did.

That night, younger brother filled a bamboo tube with cassowary oil. He put a small hole in the bottom of the tube. He hung it over older brother's sleeping place. After a while older brother said, "Rain is falling on me." Younger brother said, "No, big brother. It's all right. You stay there. That's all right." Older brother stayed there. The cassowary oil fell on him and his skin shrunk.

Afterward older brother went back to his land and found it filled with good gardens and all kinds of food. He made a big feast for his younger brother and told him to come. But the younger brother didn't come. The food was not eaten. It rotted. Younger brother's wives wanted to go back to the coast. At first younger brother did not want to go. But they were insistent. After a while younger brother went to the coast. Older brother stayed in the highlands, and all Tairora have come from him.

Pain: *Tairora and Western*

I REMEMBER VERY WELL WHEN MY NOSTRILS WERE BLED FOR the first time. Kainoba, Amay, Apam, Teba, and I all had it done at the same time. One day we were taken to the river. There were quite a few people there, mostly women, but some men, including Mando. We girls weren't sure what was going to happen and we just stood around on the riverbank not knowing what to do. Then they grabbed us. Ihua grabbed me and Taramao helped her and they pulled me into the water. They held me very tightly so I could not get away. Ihua held my hands behind my back and Taramao held my head still. I didn't like it and tried to get free of them, but they were strong women and they held on tight. Then Mando came toward me. We were all standing in the water. In his hand he held some reeds with razor-sharp edges. He told me to be quiet and be still. Taramao was holding my head so I could not move it. Mando stood in front of me, right in front of me. He looked straight at me and told me to behave. He said that this would make me strong.

Then he put the reeds in my nostrils, shoved them way up in and pulled them out and shoved them in and out, in and out. It hurt a great deal and I tried to get away but the women held me tightly. He cut and cut my nostrils and there was a lot of blood. When those reeds began to get dull he took new sharp ones and cut and cut some more. Then he took another set and cut and cut and more and more blood came. His hands were covered with blood and there was blood all over my face and it was falling down onto my chest and all over my body. My skirt was covered with blood too. We had been told to wear old skirts. I think he used six or seven sets of reeds on me. After he was finished, they let me lean over the water and the blood continued to flow out and into the water. The water became very red where I was standing.

The operation was very painful. We were told that it was good for us. They said that as we grew up it was necessary to get rid of the old blood. Everyone had to get rid of old blood from time to time. Then he would stay well and strong and do all the things he should. My whole face and nose and head ached. I wanted to get out of the water, wanted to go lie down and go to sleep, but they wouldn't let me. Then we heard other people coming. Men and women tried to come into the water and hit us. They hit us and they shouted and made a lot of noise. Taramao put her arm around me and tried to protect me from some of the blows but I was hit quite a bit.

After this was finished we were taken back to a house in the village and told to get dressed up. We put on front and back skirt panels, we put on a new belt, put red paint on our noses and around our mouths, black paint on our foreheads and cheeks. Then we all went out in front of the house where they had made an earth oven and the food was just being taken out. We were given food and then after that was all over they let us go to sleep. They told us that we should remember to cut our own nostrils in this manner from time to time. This is something that men do quite often, or they used to, but women don't do it as much after the first time. It is not as necessary for women to do it because they get rid of a lot of old blood during their monthlies and that is all right. But men do it much more.

Another thing that we learned to do to keep us strong was to beat our skin with nettles. We did this more often than we cut our nostrils. Even when I was older I would do this. I still do it sometimes if I have a sore or a swollen place. One time Teba, Kainoba, Apam, and I collected several kinds of greens and other food and went toward the Ramu River. There each of us got a big bunch of nettles. We played along the riverbank, we hit ourselves with the nettles, hit all parts of our body, arms, legs, back, chest. Then we'd sit in the hot sun for a while and after that we would run into the cold, cold water. We did this to make us strong. By evening we were very tired so we slept in a nearby house. We had gone in the water just above that. We bathed, beat our skins with nettles, sunned, cooked food, went in the water again. We stayed there and did this over and over to make ourselves strong. It was a good time. We had a lot of fun.

The sun was hot, there was no rain and we had fun. After we were finished with the nettles we threw them into the water and didn't leave them lying around on the ground because a sorcerer might come along and get them and use them to make sorcery against us. We had a good time but when we were finished we realized that we didn't have any pig grease to rub on our skin to keep it from hurting. After you hit your skin with nettles and go in the cold water, you should rub your body with pig grease so it won't hurt so much. But we didn't have any that day and as we walked home in the hot sun, our skin was uncomfortable, very painful. It really stung.

Before a girl was married she was not supposed to fuck. Before a girl first menstruated boys might try to penetrate her but most girls were afraid to do it that early. They were afraid of what boys would do to them. We were told many stories about how young boys and girls should behave toward each other. This is one of them.

Once some people sent a young boy and a young girl, both about twelve years old, to get breadfruit leaves. The boy and girl went to the forest together. The girl was going to get the leaves. She climbed up a tree to get the leaves. The boy stayed down below. He watched her climb the tree. He looked at her as she went up the tree. He saw something of hers, something which belongs to a young girl. The girl wanted to get one particular leaf. The boy said, "No, you get another one." She said, "This one?" He said, "No, that other one." They went back and forth like this. The boy telling her what one to get and the girl wanting to get another one. What the boy really wanted was to look at the girl's cunt. The boy said to her, "You put one leg on one branch and one leg you put on another branch and you get a leaf from the very top of the tree." He said this so her legs would be spread wide apart and he could get a good look at her bottom. As she did this, the boy tilted his head so he could see her cunt better. Out of the corner of her eye and girl saw him do this. She became very embarrassed. She liked the boy. She wanted to marry him. But he should not see her cunt. She came down the tree. They went back to the village and she told her mother and father what had happened. Then she said, "I like this boy. Will you let me marry him?" They said, "No, you are betrothed to someone else." The girl did not want to marry that person. She wanted to marry this boy. But her parents were stubborn.

After a while the boy got dressed up. He put his noseplug in his nose, he put on his feather headdress, he put on his shells, he put leaves in his armbands. He put on all his finery. Then he got up and he left the village. The young girl followed him. The boy said, "You go back. They will help you. They are cross with me. I am very much ashamed. You go back." The girl continued to follow him. After a while the boy gave the girl his armband and told her to take it back to the village. He said, "Your father and mother are cross with me. You have followed me. Now you go back." But the girl just took the armband and continued to follow him. In a while the boy gave her his legband and told her to take it back to the village. But she just took it, put it in her net bag and said, "No, I am going to follow you. We will go together." But the boy still wanted her to go back. He gave her all of his finery and with each thing he told her to take it back to the village. He even gave her his bamboo mouth harp. But she just put the things in her net bag. She kept following the boy.

They walked and walked and walked. They came to a woods. It was just a woods. There was no village there, there was no food. The boy had stolen taro from a garden he found along the road. One he gave to the girl and one he kept for himself. He kept stealing taro until the whole taro garden was empty. He would always steal two at a time. One he would keep for himself. One he would give to the girl.

Then the people looked at the garden. They said, "Who is stealing from the taro garden?" They put a piece of aromatic wood on the path. If the thief had walked over the wood it would end up in his village. That was how they could tell who the thief was. But the wood stayed there. Then the men went to an old woman. They said to her, "You make a little shelter of bananas leaves. You watch and see who is eating the taro. Is it a bird? Is it a possum? What is eating the taro? You watch." They said this to the old woman. So she made the shelter and she watched the garden. She saw the man come. The man counted the taro. He said, "Tomorrow the taro in this garden will be all finished." Then he went back to the woods and cooked the taro. The old woman went back to the village and told her sons, "A man came. He is good meat. He wears a red laplap. He is all dressed up."

The boy said to the girl, "One garden is finished. Another garden is almost finished. I must find another garden. If I do not come back tonight you wait for me. He talked this way and he left. The old woman had talked to the men in the village and they all waited in a third garden. When the boy came all the men saw him. They all shot arrows at him. They killed him and cut him into pieces. Then they cooked him and ate him up.

That evening the boy did not come back to the woods. The girl wanted to sleep. A ghost got the bones of the boy, brought them back to the woods, cooked them, and ate them. The girl saw this. She just watched. She stayed very still. She didn't make any noise. She watched the spirit cook food and the bones. She watched the spirit eat. The spirit ate the boy's bones. The woman shit and pissed. She did lots of things but she didn't make any noise. She stayed very, very still. Then the girl got up and took a drum. She saw the spirit and the bones and left. The spirit followed her. He did not follow close. Just close enough so he could hear the drum as she beat it.

She went back to her parent's village. Soon the spirit called to her from a nearby mountain and told her to come. He pretended to be her husband. When people asked her why she didn't go she said, "They killed my husband. He stole taro from their garden. All the people killed him. Only his spirit is there." The spirit said "You come and the two of us will go up on that mountain. I'll go first. I'll wait there for you. You come afterward." The spirit talked this way.

Soon the girl died. She followed the boy and they lived in the place of the spirits. This is the story we were told when we were young. We were told that it was no good for a girl and boy to be familiar with each other before marriage. If they did there would be serious trouble afterward. They might die. They should wait until the proper time to be familiar. Should wait until after the girl gets new skirts. Until after she has given her husband food.

But when I was young, if boys liked us we could cuddle with them and we used to do it a lot. There was nothing wrong with it. We could do this until we were married but then we were not supposed to do it any more. Boys could keep on cuddling with other girls, even after they were married. After a woman had her first baby, though, her husband was supposed to stop cuddling other girls because this meant that now he was a man, no longer a boy. Now he should behave like a man.

When we began to cuddle with the boys we would do it out in the tall grass sometimes but most often we would do it at night at the girls' house. A lot of girls slept there instead of in their mothers' houses, others would sleep there sometimes but sometimes just spend the evening and then go back to their mother's house to sleep. If we wanted to cuddle with a particular boy we would have a close girlfriend tell him. Some time during the day she would tell him that her friend wanted to cuddle with him. That he should come to the girls' house that night. If he liked the girl and wanted to cuddle with her he would come. First of all after he arrived at the girls' house he would sit by the fire and warm himself. There were two rooms in the girls' house, an outer room with a fire burning in it, and an inner room with mats on the floor or raised woven bamboo platforms to lie on. One of the boys I used to cuddle with would always play his bamboo mouth harp for a while. All of us would sit around the fire, talking and laughing. After a while we would go into the inner room and lie down and cuddle, sometimes for a long time, sometimes not.

We would lie beside each other. Sometimes I would put my head on his arm and sometimes he would put his on mine. Then we would rub our cheeks and jaws together, back and forth, back and forth. We could cuddle in this way. Usually we girls would take off some of our skirts but we were always sure to keep on at least one long panel in front and one in back, long enough so the two panels would meet between our legs. We didn't want the boy to be able to get at our parts. The boys after they had been cuddling awhile would want to do this. But we knew we were not supposed to let them and we didn't.

If I liked the boy a lot I would put my arm out in a bent fashion so it would make a good pillow for his head and he would be comfortable. If I didn't like him very much I would leave my arm straight; this wasn't as comfortable for him as if I'd bent my elbow. The boys knew that we were frightened of them, frightened that they would want to fuck us and so some of them always stayed very still. That is, they kept their bodies rigid. Wouldn't move their arms or legs, not even to scratch a louse. They knew that if they started to move we would think they were thinking about fucking and that we would get scared and stop cuddling with them.

Sometimes my girl friend would lie with us and she would kill any lice that might be biting him. I would do the same for her when she was cuddling with a boy. We all cuddled in the same room. Sometimes everyone was cuddling with a boy but often, most of the time in fact, there would be some girls who wouldn't have boys to cuddle and they would tend the fire and help us in other ways.

There were some boys who were always trying to fuck and usually if one did, we would tell our parents, our father or our brother. These boys wanted to put their hands under our skirts and play with our parts. Some of the girls would let them do this because they liked the feel of it. But we had been told that it was not good to do this. And most girls did not. We were told that no one was ever to see our genitals. Little girls wear skirts in the front from the time they are very young and a girl learns to hide her genitals from everyone. It's all right to see boys' cocks and balls and even men do not hide theirs very well, so girls know what men are like. But they are not supposed to see our genitals. I cuddled with many boys when I was young but only two that I did it with very much.

Both of them are dead now, but I liked them a lot although I was not engaged to either one.

Some boys and girls fucked all the time. If a boy tried it and the girl let him, she might like it so much that she would go on and on with it. Sometimes someone would know what they were doing and they'd threaten to tell the girl's parents or brother if she and her boyfriend didn't give them something or do favors for them. Most girls that did this didn't become pregnant. But sometimes it would happen. Sometimes it would happen and the girl wouldn't really know that it had happened until some older woman noticed that she hadn't menstruated for a while and then she would tell her that she was pregnant. She was asked, "Whose child are you carrying?" If the girl told, then her parents would try to get the boy to marry her as soon as possible. Sometimes, though, the girl was already indicated for another boy and maybe some pay had already been given and they would try to get this boy to go through the betrothal ceremony quickly. After that she would give him cooked food much sooner than an ordinary girl would, so that when the baby was born they would already be really married.

But girls who hadn't menstruated usually didn't have intercourse and not all of those girls who had menstruated did it before they were married or with boys they weren't going to marry. The older girls knew that they might get pregnant. They didn't want to. But most of them didn't know anything to eat or chew to keep them from getting pregnant. Married women knew that but not the girls. But if a girl liked a boy and fucked with him they would often try to get their parents to let them marry sooner than would ordinarily be the case.

Some of the time when I was young there was no girls' house and a lot of us girls lived together at the house of Ikat and his two wives, Titia and Kora. Kora's children all died when they were young, but Titia had two daughters. Ten of us, including Teba, Kainoba, Apam, Amay, and me, sometimes lived at this house. Long ago, long before I was born, there was no separate girls' house. It was only later that some of the villages had a girls' house. They learned about it from other people, from the Kamano I think.

As the old women tell you, there was no girls' house when they were young. When I was young we didn't always have one. And as I am now telling you, some of the time when I was a young girl, before I was married, we stayed with Ikat's two wives. They were good people, kind people, and they liked to have us there. Ikat built a big house for his wives. There were two hearths in it, one hearth belonged to Titia and one belonged to Kora. We girls would divide up between these two fires.

We spent our evenings there and we slept there. We worked for them: we fetched firewood and water for them and helped them in the gardens. We also had gardens of our own in which we worked. Also, if Ikat and his wives started some sort of task, we would help them and sometimes finish it for them. They were generous and very good to us. They gave us some food, although we still got food from our mothers and fathers. They gave us pig grease to rub on our skirts and on our bodies.

Ikat gave us rats to eat. He kept traps set in the long grass near the house so he caught quite a few rats and gave them to us. He made traps like the ones in back of your house. Made them of two pieces of bamboo fastened with a bamboo string. He also set quite a few traps in his gardens. He liked to set traps and catch rats and he gave most of them to us girls to eat. We got along quite well. Ikat usually was good to both wives, and the two women did not fight much with each other. But they did fight sometimes and occasionally they used their fighting sticks although I didn't see any very serious injuries.

Titia and Kora were good workers and always took good care of their pigs. A few women were lazy and didn't look after their gardens well or take good care of their pigs. Most women, however, fed them good food and looked after them well. If a woman was given a baby pig or if a sow died after having a piglet, the woman would let the pig drink her milk. She would hold the piglet so it could suckle at her breast. She carried the pig around in her net bag just as she would carry a baby. I have never let a pig suck at my breast. A baby pig has teeth and I think it would hurt. If I had to do it, I would not watch the pig sucking at my breast because I think it would hurt and I would not want to watch. Also, the snout of the pig pushing in and up and down would not feel good, I think. But some women did this.

Also a woman would put a rope around the leg of a little pig and lead it around. She did this so it would not run away. Pigs try to run away, and when the pig is little its owner must look after it well. Sometimes pigs would run away. When a woman discovered this she had to look for it until she found it. You remember seeing Ate the other day. Even though it was raining hard and it was cold outside, she spent a lot of time looking for her pig. She called it and called it. Women know how to call pigs and if a pig hears he will come to her to be fed. It was a very cold day so Ate wore a bark cape and held her arms across her chest to help her keep warm.

Later, a woman cut the pig's tail and also made cuts in its ears so that everyone would know that it was her pig. If someone tried to steal it she could tell which pig was hers. When a male pig gets big he will want to mount female pigs. If he does this often he will not grow; he will remain skin and bones. Because of this a woman castrates her pig. A man or woman cuts the balls off with a bamboo knife. The pigs squeal because it hurts them. Women watch their pigs closely and let them mount some female pigs because they want to have more pigs. But they do not let them do it all the time. If a pig gets sick and dies the woman drags an old net bag back and forth over it. This will keep her other pigs from getting sick or lost. Titia and Kora used to take good care of their pigs and we helped them.

There was another house that some of us sometimes went to in the evening. Aruna lived at Abiera when I was young and we girls would often go there for the evening. We would talk about a lot of things, laugh, joke, and have a good time. One night when we girls were there alone we were talking about fucking, men's genitals, and that sort of thing. I even took a stick and drew a picture on the ground and said, "That's a cock, that's the balls." We were talking about these things and some men must have come near the house and heard us. I don't remember how loud we were talking or if we heard anyone outside. I don't remember any of that. There were no men inside the house with us. But some men heard us and they became very angry and wanted all the men to come from the men's house and punish us.

We heard them call out to the men in the men's house to tell them to come and beat us. We were very frightened because they wanted to take us out of Aruna's house one at the time and give each of us a good beating. So we sneaked out, one by one, and we all got away into the tall grass before they could catch us. We were gone before they realized it, and that made them even madder. All of us went in different directions and we planned to meet again later that night. Usually we would be afraid to run around alone at night but that time we were so scared of being beaten by the men that we didn't even think about it.

We decided to meet and then we would all go together over into Kamano territory, where the men would not get us. They would be afraid to go there because the Kamano were enemies. We would be safe there. A friend of my mother's brother lived in a Kamano village and I knew he would help us. He would let us stay there and then after the men were no longer angry with us we could come back to Abiera. We would all join each other and then we would go to Kamano territory together. It wouldn't be good for the men to find us while they were so angry.

So we all met and then we climbed the big hill, went through the woods and down on the other side to the Lutheran mission station. We slept there. In the morning we went to the church service. My uncle's friend was there and he said, "What are you doing here?" We lied to him and told him that the parents of one of my friends wanted her to marry a boy she didn't like and that we had all run away with her. We knew that the men would not come this far to get us. But we knew that we couldn't stay here very long.

So the next day we started back to Abiera. I was about twelve years old at the time. We started out all together and we played and fooled around at first. We spent some time sliding down the grassy hillsides. We would lift up our skirts and slide along on our buttocks. We did this for a while and then as time went on we split up into small groups. We saw an earth oven cooking in the distance but we didn't go near it. We kept well hidden in the long grass. That night we didn't go back to Abiera. We slept at Aja's house at Bahiora. We didn't go back to Abiera.

The next morning we got up early and when we got near Tagantira we saw Aruna and Ikat tightening their bows. They were still mad at us and wanted to go out and find us so we could be punished. This frightened us all the more. We hid in the woods. We went to the woods, like cows move around, one by one and not all in a close group. One by one we went to the woods to hide, at least that was the plan. But Kainoba stayed hidden in the tall grass. At least she thought she was hidden but she wasn't hidden very well. The men found her, hit her with big sticks, and then sent her back to Abiera. The men kept looking and they found some of the girls and chased the rest of us. We would go some place and hide. They would look for us. If they began to get near we would run off, very quietly, and when the men got there we would be gone. They got madder and madder.

Finally I became separated from most of my friends. That night I hid in the reeds down near a little house that Ikat used for watching rats when he was hunting them. The ground was damp and I stayed in the same position all night so that my skirt was damp in the morning and my legs and arms were stiff. Teba was still with me. In the morning she went to a garden to get some food and she was caught. The men made her tell where I was but by then I had moved and they didn't find me.

I ran to Bano's pig house and stayed there for a while. At Bano's house I sat down and cried. I had lost my net bag. I told Bano I had lost one of my skirts and that I was looking for it and had come there to look. Ioga asked me where I was going when I left and I said I was going to look for my skirt. He urged me to stay and eat and said that then I could go find my skirt. I told him, "It's no good for me to stay here and get caught. I must go to another place." But Ioga still told me to stay and eat. He knew the truth of what had happened. "If they come here to get you I can fight them. You don't have to be afraid here." So I stayed there and ate and then I went back to Aja's house. There I learned what had happened to some of the other girls and I cried. I cried when I thought about them, Teba particularly.

She was older than me. When all of this happened she was not married but she was engaged to Bauno. He was very, very angry with her because she had been such a bighead during all of this. He was so angry that he shot her with three arrows, once in the right breast, once in the calf, and once in the thigh. He was very, very angry with her and he shot her three times. But I knew I could not stay at Aja's forever, so I started back to Aruna's house at Abiera. I crept in there and no one saw me. I entered the house and hid under a pandanus mat.

They were talking about me; they all wondered where I was. They were quite concerned and Aruna said he would go out and look for me again; he would take his bow and arrow and go find me. I don't think he really would have shot me, he just wanted to take the bow and arrow with him. Men liked to carry their bow and arrows with them when they walked about.

Aruna's wife told him he should go and go soon, right away, but Aruna said it was going to rain and he didn't want to go and get wet, so he would wait until the next day. His wife said, "No, you go now. You should find her now." However, Aruna insisted that he sleep now and he would go tomorrow after the rain had come and gone.

In a short while I came out from under the mat. At first everyone was very surprised and in the dim light they weren't sure who it was and I had to tell them twice. I cried and cried and Aruna's wife did too. They were all glad to see me. I said, "Yes, I've come back." During all of this I was away for four or five nights. I was the only one of the girls who was not caught. Kainoba was away two nights before she was caught. She was the first one who was caught.

I did not get any punishment. Aruna was glad to see me; he was no longer angry. His wives, too, were very glad to see me and they weren't at all angry with me. I guess the men had gotten so mad at us because they thought we were too young to be talking so frankly and freely about sexual matters. They had been listening to us and I guess when I drew the picture of the genitals and said what they were out loud, the men got really angry and thought we needed to be punished. They thought that we had been bigheads for too long and that we needed some punishment. When they heard us that night they got really angry at us.

We used to have different ways of treating illness. One thing was always done if a person had ringworm. A frog and a certain kind of leaf were cooked together in a bamboo tube. They were put in the tube and the tube was roasted in the fire. After the food was cooked the person with the ringworm ate some of it and the rest was rubbed on his skin. This would cure him. For many kinds of sores and sickness we chewed leaves. A man chewed some leaves and gingerroot and then he spit this on a sick person. Or he spat this on the food that the sick person was going to eat. This was done often.

If a person was really sick a pig was killed. Both the blood and fat of the pig were rubbed on his body. Usually someone chewed leaves and gingerroot and spat this into the pig blood before it was rubbed on the body. The sick person would also be given some pig meat to eat. It couldn't be a pig of his; it had to be a pig belonging to someone else. The blood that was rubbed on his body could be from one of his own pigs but he could not eat his own pig.

We all had some kinds of sores when I was a young girl. Most of us girls would get sores on our hips where the strings of our skirts passed over them. Some girls had them worse than others. Meruka used to have great big ones. Some girls would scratch them too. They itched a lot. The itching could drive us crazy. If a girl scratched them they would get bigger. After a girl got married they usually disappeared because a woman's skirts don't cut into the skin.

Some people used to have sores on their faces that stayed forever. Have you seen Ihabi at Ehubajra? She had big, big sores and after a while her nose got smaller and her mouth got bigger. The sores were eating the skin. Then a doctor came and gave her a shot and the sores went away. She still looks different though. Part of her nose is gone and also part of her mouth. I guess that very long ago there were people who had this and they died from it. I have heard stories about some people who got so bad that they smelled bad too. Then they had to live all alone in a house which was away from the village. No one wanted to be near them because they smelled so bad. I didn't know anyone like that but I've heard stories. We had no medicine for those sores, but the White man can give a shot to cure them.[4]

I told you that when I was sick they cut me so I would bleed a lot. We believe that when a person has certain illnesses it is because he has too much blood or bad blood. Most illness is caused by sorcery, but some is just sickness alone. No sorcery is done but the illness just comes. It can be from the spirit of another person. The person is cross with you and his spirit comes to make you sick. Or we think it can come because a person has too much blood. So one thing that we do is to bleed a sick person. Sometimes the skin over the ribs is cut. Sometimes the skin on the head near the hairline is cut. This is often done for headaches. We used to use a bamboo knife or a sharp piece of black stone. But today a piece of broken glass or a razor may be used, although for some sicknesses the black shiny stone is still the best.

If your leg pains, you can be cut in the leg. You saw us treat Iroa when he had a bad knee. This is the old way of doing it. He twisted his knee when he stepped in a garden ditch. His knee was very sore and painful and it hurt him to walk. It did not get better so he wanted to get rid of some of his blood. Amata took a little bow and shot arrows into Iroa's leg. He shot them where he could see the vein. Shot him many times. I helped by pressing on Iroa's leg so a lot of blood would come out. When I was young we did this for many things. If we had a toothache someone would shoot small arrows at our face or jaw so we would bleed. Many people still do this. Pina sometimes shoots the face of Ubaj's baby to make it get well. But the baby has a big sickness and does not get well.

We don't know why. The baby's father killed a snake. Maybe now the spirit of the snake is on the baby's skin. Or was it caused by the water when the baby was baptized? Or maybe it got something at the infirmary. We really don't know.

I didn't know much about our medicine and curing when I was a girl. I learned the things I've told you. Everybody knew these things. But I did not learn anything more about curing sickness. There were people who could cure illness but I didn't know much about this. Some of them lived in other areas and they would come here to cure someone who was quite ill. There are still people like this among the Tairora. Arat tries to be a curer but she is not very good. She has not cured any really sick people. The ones she has cured were not very sick to begin with. Arat talks a lot about the witchcraft she knows, but I don't believe it.

One afternoon a few weeks ago when she was visiting here I was going down to the river to take my bath. She wanted to go with me so I said, "All right, you can come." We went down together and when we got there I put my clothes in a pile and put a safety pin on top of them. I jumped in the water and took my bath. Arat did not take a bath, but stayed on the bank and we talked. When I came out of the water to get my clothes the pin was gone. I thought it must have dropped into the water. Arat said she thought that was what happened too.

The water was very muddy and we couldn't see where the pin was. Arat told me that she would make the water clear up where the pin had fallen so we could see it and get it back. She told me to call out to my ancestors. I did. Arat called out to them too. Then she said some other things. She moved her hands round over the water while she talked. Then she leaned over, put her hand in the water, and brought out the pin.

She said that she had called to our ancestors and they had made the water clear in the place where the pin was. Then she took it out. But I didn't believe her. I don't think she can do this. I think that she took the pin when I was in the water and wasn't looking at her. Then she hid it. After she worked her magic she brought the pin out and pretended she had found it in the water. That's what I think she did.

One thing I should tell you about is the first White man that came here. The first one that I remember is Johannes. I remember when he first came here. He made his Lutheran station at Onarunka over across the Ramu River from here. It was on Kamano land. The station was there for a long time. During the war (World War II) it was abandoned, and when Johannes came back after the war he built the new station at Raipinka where it is today. I did not know much about the mission when I was young. I was not baptized then and I did not go over to the mission except for a few times.

Johannes was the first White man I remember seeing, but my father told me that another White man came into this area before Johannes came. He was called Mata Karu. He came from the Markham River Valley to Arau. He had a map with names on it. At Arau he asked, "Is so-and-so at Barabuna?" They answered, "Yes." So he went to Barabuna. There he asked, "Is so-and-so at Noreikora?" and they said "Yes." So he went there. There he asked if Matoto was here at Tairora and when they said "Yes," he came over here. After he left here he went to Goroka and to Chimbu. Then later he came back. This man was blind in one eye. After he had left here the mission came. I don't know if this man belonged to the mission or what he belonged to. I don't really remember him although I think I remember the excitement and talk when he came into the area.

After Johannes came we would see him sometimes because he would go back and forth from his station to the Markham River. He would cross our land. We were not afraid of Johannes but we were afraid of some of the other early White men that we knew. We were very much afraid of some of the government bosses because they did so many things to harm us. Then too we heard stories of some of them who did very bad things to some New Guineans we knew.

One time when the *kiap* came to get us we all ran away from the village as fast as we could. I was still a young girl then. I ran as fast and as far as I could and then I hid among some reeds in low ground. But my feet were not completely hidden and a policeman came by and saw them. He grabbed me by the arm and pulled me out to see if I was a girl or boy. When he saw I was a girl he took me to the house where they were keeping all of the people they caught. If I had been a boy I would have been shot. That time when the *kiap* came after us ten men and two boys were shot. This was one time in my life when I was most frightened. When I was small and the men would get angry at us, like the time we were bigheading too much about sex, I would be frightened, but never as much as when the White men came after us.

In the early days when the *kiap* was here one of the troubles was that we locals didn't know very much Pidgin. Often the men, or any of us, wouldn't really understand what was being said to us. Then we might do the wrong thing, not because we wanted to but because we didn't know what was being said to us. Sometimes too they would ask us to do things but because we didn't understand we didn't do them. This would make them very angry with us and they would do brutal things—hit people, chase them, kill them. At that time the native New Guinean policemen were all from coastal areas and they didn't speak our language. There were no translators then.

We were not the only people who were killed by the *kiap*s and we knew about some of the others. One time, a *kiap* was angry with a man from Noreikora. The *kiap* told the people to make a big earth oven. Then he put the man on the earth oven. The man was cooked alive. He wasn't killed first but he did die. I was in Kainantu when this happened and I saw the corpse when they brought it into Kainantu. The meat was gone from the bones—we could see the bone in some places through the flesh. The son of this man still lives at Noreikora, and he is angry still with the government for having killed his father.

One Rite After Another

FTER THE WHITE MAN CAME, THE GOVERNMENT MADE new leaders for us. They were called *luluai* and *tultul*. These were to be our head men even though they might not be the most important men in the village. Each *luluai* and *tultul* was given a cap to wear on his head and a medal to hang around his neck. He could keep these as long as the government wanted him to hold the office. Ointa was our first *luluai*. After that, Bano was made a *luluai*. Later on Ointa's hat went to Ara'u, the albino. After it was taken away from him it went to Komo, who still has it. And afterward Ara'u got another cap, the one at Noreikora. These men got their hats and they got the medal that they wear around their necks.

Bano was *luluai* for a long time, but after a while the *kiap* got cross with him and Bano was cross with the *kiap*. Bano's son Akua was arrested and Bano didn't think he should be. I don't remember what it was for. But Bano complained to the *kiap* and then the *kiap* said Bano was not a good *luluai*—that he didn't do his job well, that he didn't take the job seriously. He said Bano brought cases to court in Kainantu too often and that many of the cases he brought were unimportant and should have been settled by him in the village.

Bano turned in his hat then because the *kiap* was treating the people so badly. Bano said, "The *kiap* rounds us up and treats us like animals. We are not dogs and pigs and we shouldn't be treated that way." So the *kiap* put Bano in jail. Akua, his son, was there too and the two of them were chained to each other. They wore metal collars and there was a chain between the collars of Bano and Akua.

In those days the prisoners in jail at Kainantu were kept in small round houses made of thatch. There was a fence around the area. Bano got a stick and when the guard was not there he would dig around one of the fence posts until he had it loosened so he could lift it and the wire fence a bit and get out. He finally did get out and he was not caught by the *kiap*. He came back to the village.

It was quite a while after I had seen a few White men out here that I went into Kainantu for the first time. I was about eleven years old I guess. I walked in with several people from here. At that time there were some New Guineans working on the old airstrip that was over where the agricultural office is now. There was also an airplane there.

It was the first time I had seen an airplane. We went over to see the workmen and also to see the plane. I wondered what the plane was like. Did it have guts? Did it piss? Did it shit? Did it know how to eat? What was that round thing in front? Was it an eye? Was it like a pig? Could it walk? These were some of the things I wondered when I first saw the plane. We approached it very slowly and carefully. We wanted to see as much as we could but we were also a little bit afraid because we didn't know just what sort of thing it was. That time I did not go near enough to the plane to touch it or to look inside of it, but I looked into it as hard as I could from a distance. At that time, too, I didn't know that a man had to make it go. I thought the plane could fly by itself.

It was one time after this when the *kiap* came down here with policemen. I don't know why they came. It was after fighting time was over. But it was before the Japanese came. I don't think they were looking for Japanese. I'm not sure why they came at us. But they came and most of the people ran away to the woods to hide. Bano's first wife, Aruo, thought she hid too. But she had very poor eyesight then (she is blind now), and although she could still see things that were near to her she couldn't see anything that was away from her. She hid in the reeds. But she did not hide well enough and she could not see someone coming toward her. Even when he came fairly close to her she was not sure if it was a policeman or the *kiap*. It was a policeman from Anona. He took her net bag, took her knife, took everything that was in the net bag and then he shot her with his gun. The bullet hit her leg and then went through her arm—she was crouching down when he shot her. Her leg was hurt and her arm was very badly wounded. The arm did not fall off, it just hung down loosely at her side if she did not hold it with the other hand. She could not see well enough to go and find help.

Finally Bano found her. He could not move her. She was too badly hurt to walk and he could not carry her far away where most of the people were hiding. So he moved her to a better hiding place and he covered her with grass and with a pandanus mat. This kept the sun from burning her too much and the rain from hitting her. She had no fire so she got cold at night. But it was dangerous for anyone to stay with her because the police and the *kiap* were still looking for people in the area and everyone was hiding. Bano would bring food to her. He would sneak to her by one path and then he would leave by another. He would crouch down and sneak through the tall grass to take food to her.

She was very sick. After a while, before people went back to the village, he built a small house for her over near Ehubajra and somehow got her to that house. I don't know how he did it but he did. Then she stayed there for a long time. As she got better she could keep a fire going, cook food, and do things like that. But it took a long time for her arm to get well. You have seen it now. It is much shorter than her other arm and the upper part is very big around. It is not like a regular arm at all. For a long while it hung limply and she could do nothing with it. It did get a little bit stronger after it healed. But she never could work with that arm.

Several times during the big war (World War II), everyone ran away from the village. Soldiers came here and had a station up on top of the mountain near Kambuta. They lived in the woods by Kambuta and over the ridge from it. It was a big woods then. There were a lot of soldiers and they lived in round thatch huts which they built fairly close to one another; they were crowded together. They used up a lot of our trees and firewood so now the forest is very small. It used to be much bigger.

The soldiers wanted us to stay here but most of us left—not all at once, but some would go one time, some would go another time. We sneaked away because we didn't want the soldiers to catch us leaving, as they didn't want us to go. We were afraid because some soldiers and policemen had come before and broken and burned our bows and arrows. We were afraid of them and so we didn't want to stay. Bano's people went south, down to Arogara. Other groups went southwest, some to Ontenu. Mando's line went to the Kamano and I went with them. Afterward, when we came back, not all of the people who had left returned. Some of Bano's line went to Ehubajra and they are still there.

During this time some bombs fell in this area and one of them killed Esias, a woman from Anona. The planes would also drop a lot of food. We could see the men open the door of the airplane and see them pushing cargo out the door. Sometimes we found the food; if we did we would hide it and then go out and bring in a little bit at a time when we needed it. We sometimes found rice, canned meat, and other things.[5]

When the first bomb fell, the soldiers were living up the mountainside at Kambuta. After the soldiers went away we returned to the village. Then the *kiap* came and asked us if we had seen any Japanese soldiers. We hadn't but he was mean to us anyway and a lot of people left again this time. The *kiap* asked one man who was working in his garden down near Abiera if he had seen Japanese soldiers. He replied, "No." The *kiap* took a man from Ontabura with him to Noreikora, when they were looking for Japanese. While they were there he killed the Ontabura. He was angry because they weren't finding any Japanese and he thought the man from Ontabura and the others were not telling the truth when they said they didn't know where any Japanese were. Ebu avenged this killing by killing a policeman just a short while after this.

I remember another time during the war when several policemen were in our area searching for Japanese soldiers. The policemen tried to get all the people together in one place but some of the people got away. That day they were burning grass at Toagura and some of us were hunting rats. When the policemen came we ran away, ran in all directions. A lot of people were caught. I wasn't, although I was all alone. I hid by the path at first, then I slowly slid along the ground and got in a ditch. I crouched along it and finally got to an old burial place that was covered with grass.

The police were looking for me and they got close, but a spirit was affecting their eyes and they didn't see me. Then they gave up and left. I got up and looked around. I saw one person in the distance but couldn't tell who it was. I was all alone. I later learned that the people the police captured were kept for a day and the next day were set free. Two of the people who hid were caught and shot by the policemen.

As I said, I was all alone so I stole down the mountainside and crossed the river at Urala. I kept thinking, "What am I going to do? What should I do? Where should I go?" So I decided to go to Arogara where my mother, Aruo, was living. I was very scared, terribly scared, but I knew I had to do something and I decided to go to Arogara.

I thought, "If I pretend I am a man I will have a better chance of not getting caught than if I look like a girl." So I took off my front and back skirts and just left the short front panel on so I would be covered. I rolled my skirts up and put them under my arm as if I were carrying a lime gourd. Then I took my net bag and hung it on my shoulder as a man would to it, not over my forehead as a woman does. I got a long stick and broke some reeds and carried these as if they were bow and arrows and I started walking to the south.

I later learned that Apam and Teba had also escaped and they were hiding in long grass just down below Ampe's present house. They saw me but they didn't recognize me. They saw a "man" walking along the other side of the river. At first they thought it was Pina and they were going to attract his attention and try to catch up with him. But then Apam decided it wasn't Pina and that they'd better be careful and not call out to a stranger. Teba still thought it was Pina and wanted to call him. But Apam was stubborn and she won and they didn't call out.

Finally, I reached Arogara. It still had a palisade around it. Villages always used to have high palisades of wooden posts around them to protect them from enemies. Although by then we no longer had a palisade at our village, Arogara still did. Ontenu did too. That village was up in the forest near the top of the mountain and it was palisaded. Later they moved down to lower ground and the new village did not have a palisade.

The palisade at Arogara had one door. There was a high platform just inside on which a guard stood. Most palisades had lookouts at the back side too, although there was no door there. That day Tunanao was on the platform inside the palisade. He was hiding and trying to catch some birds. I went up to the door and cleared my throat once. This is how we attract people's attention, by clearing our throat. He asked me what I wanted. When I told him, he asked someone to open the door for me. The door consisted of double upright poles at either side between which slats or rough planks of wood were laid, one on top of the other. To open the door the slats had to be taken out over the tops of the poles. You know how this kind of door works, since Mando still has one at his house.

While I was at Arogara, Tunanao asked me where my father was. I told him I didn't know where Mando was. He said, "No, I mean Bano. He is your true father." This was the first time I heard Bano called my father. I told Tunanao I didn't know where Bano was. I stayed at Arogara one night and the next day I returned to my village. On the way I met Apam and Teba. We stopped to roast some pandanus nuts. We compared notes on what we had done after we escaped the police. Apam and Teba were very surprised that it was I they had seen. They agreed I had done a good job of imitating a man. I walked like a man and carried things like a man does. They wondered though why I hadn't called out to them or come over to get them. But I really hadn't seen them. If I had, I would have called to them or gone to them. I was all alone and I was very frightened to be walking so far by myself.

During the no good time (World War II), we did see a few Japanese. One of them lived in a house at Barapatarera for a while. He would go up on the hills and look through binoculars all the time. Every day he would go up and look for a long time. He and some other Japanese soldiers were in an airplane that crashed in Fore country. He came up this way on foot and stayed at Barapatarera for a while. Then he rejoined his comrades and they left.

Of all of us girls, Teba, who was betrothed to Bawno for a long time, was the first to be married. She was quite young when she was betrothed. Apam was the next one married, to Komo, Amay and I were next. Later Hibii, who is now the *tultul* at Bontaa, pulled Kamando's sister, Apari, away by *hampu*.[6] Apari was indicated for someone else but Hibii liked her and wanted to marry her. Their parents did not want them to marry each other. They were very stubborn about it; they wouldn't let the two marry. So Hibii and his brothers and cousins and other young men, made magic and lured Apari away. She heard the singing. She liked it, ran away, and married Hibii.

The first time I was married I was quite young. I had not yet menstruated. Years ago girls were often married when they were very young. Some of them were very, very young when they were indicated for their husband to be. That is, a girl's father would decide whom she was to marry and from that time on she would know who her husband would be. I was indicated for Titio, a man who was a lot older than I, a man I hardly knew. His father was a Tairora. After he died, Titio's mother, an Agarabi, returned to Anona to live and Titio went with her. I didn't know Titio well. He was much older than I. I had other boy friends, other boys with whom I cuddled. Baga and I were very fond of each other and we wanted to get married. But Mando wanted me to marry Titio, and his decision was followed. He was a stubborn man. I wondered why Mando was giving me to Titio. I hardly knew him. We had not been friends, and he was much older than I.

I wondered if it was because Titio's family was going to give my family a big payment for me, or just what was it? Mando said, "We who live down here don't know how to speak Pidgin. You go to Anona. There they know how to talk Pidgin. They know all about it. You go to Anona and you learn how to talk Pidgin and after that you can serve as our interpreter." This is what Mando said but I didn't know if it was the real reason. I did know, though, that I didn't want to marry Titio, that I wanted to marry my friend Baga, at Ontabura. Mando was insistent, though, and I was betrothed to Titio.

The day the marriage was to take place was a big day in the village. Both Amay and I were being married. We were having new skirts put on us and there were to be big feasts. A lot of people came. Relatives came from many places to see me being given to Titio and also to see Amay. She and I had been close friends from the time we were small girls; our mothers had said that we were special friends. And now we were to be married on the same day.

I was all dressed up for the occasion. I still wore my hair in the old fashion with many tiny braids. Our hair does not grow very long. One thing we used to do was this. Pieces of bark string were braided with the hair to make it longer. On some men it hung down to their shoulders. That day my hair was trimmed with a bamboo knife, then it was covered with pig grease and the braids were made. As my hair was braided some decorations were put in. I remember that dog teeth were hung from some of the braids, and one dracaena leaf was bent and put in my hair. A lot of pig grease was smeared on my face as well as in my hair.

After I was all dressed up, I was taken out in front of the house. There was a pandanus mat on the ground and I stood on it. Everyone was watching me and I was very embarrassed. I was embarrassed because I was very young. I didn't like to have everyone watching me. I was also very unhappy because I didn't really want to get married yet. I was too young, just a young girl. And I did not want to marry Titio. I hardly knew him and he was much older than I was. He was a grown man and I was only a young girl. I had not yet menstruated. When Marabeba and Nagaraj brought me out to the pandanus mat, Titio was there. I put my finger inside his belt for a moment. Then he left. He was not there for the rest of the ceremony and he could not eat any of the food from the feast.

I stood on the pandanus mat and I hung my head and held my arms up to cover my face. I was very worried. What would it be like living at Anona? I didn't know what to expect. I was almost hysterical and I cried a great deal. While I was waiting on the pandanus mat, I tried to run away. I dashed off and ran up the hill to a bent tree which is still there. Gamu came after me, caught me, and took me back. I tried to run away only once; after Gamu brought me back I remained on the mat. But I didn't want to get married. I was too young.

While I stood on the mat, my mothers, Ihua and Taramao, put new skirts on me. There were ten new skirts of which Ihua and Taramao had made seven. Ampe, my sister, made one, Anta, another older sister made another, and Oivi of Anona made one. In all there were ten new skirts. The women put them on me one by one. Each skirt was made of bark strips, strips of the inner bark of a small tree. They were smeared with pig grease so the skirts were very heavy. After the first one had been put on, Ihua reached up under it and took off my old girl's skirt; but the small pubic panel remained. The new skirts were different from the old skirts. The new ones covered me all the way around, covering the sides of my legs as the old ones had not. Also these skirts were much heavier than the old ones. The last one to be put on, the top one, was a bit longer than the others. Putting on these new skirts was the same as putting a ring on my finger today. It meant that now I was a married woman.

These skirts were very heavy. After they were on, a long strip of bark cloth, which was tied to the back of the outer skirt, was released and one end fell to the ground. Then my brother stood in front of me with his back to me. He bent forward, reached backward between his legs, grabbed the bark cloth strip, pulled it forward, and cut it. It was a brother's job to cut the bark strip so I would be free to go to my husband's family. My own family was giving me to my husband's family.

After the skirts were on, Mando stood up and gave a long speech. He told everyone what a good girl I was. He said that I would work hard, that our people were good people and did things well. Titio's stepfather talked too, as did some other men. There was a lot of talk. When the speeches were finished Mando gave me two new net bags, a new metal knife, and a small female pig. In the old days a girl might be given a stone adze and wooden bowls. I have heard that sometimes a newly married girl was given a bow and arrows to give to her husband. But I'm not sure about this. I took only two net bags, a steel knife, and the sow with me.

I was unhappy during the whole time. I thought about running away and I did try it once. I thought I would run and tell the *kiap* about it. I even thought of tearing off the new skirts and throwing them away. But finally I decided that I wouldn't do these things but that I would go with my husband's family as I was supposed to do. I did not behave very well and some people were cross with me because I did not behave better. Ehaa was very cross with me and scolded me several times. That made me angry. After the ceremony was finished I was still angry with her and I wanted to fight with her.

I ran to the house, got a fighting stick that was up in the roof thatch, and ran out to fight with Ehaa. We shouted at each other, danced around, and called each other names. I did most of this because Ehaa didn't really want to fight. She was cross with me because of the way I had behaved and she had bawled me out a lot. This made me angry and made me want to fight with her, but she really didn't want to fight. I threatened her and called her names. I really wanted to fight. I hit her hard on the head several times. Her scalp was cut, her hair was torn off, and she began to bleed. But she still didn't want to fight and she didn't hit back. Finally, Bori took me by the wrists and made me stop fighting. But I was very angry with Ehaa because of what she said to me about my behavior at that time. I didn't want to get married, not to Titio. I was very upset about it all.

I was married at Bahiora and I stayed there for two nights before Ohi, Titio's sister-in-law took me to Anona. The day we started I was wearing all of my skirts, but they were so heavy that they began to slip down. I tried to hold them up with my hands, both in front and in back, but it was very embarrassing, as I thought they were all going to fall off at once and I would be naked in front of people. So I took off six skirts and wore four to Anona. Ohi was in charge of taking me to Anona, although other people went along with us. We left Bahiora and started toward Anona.

When we got near Bititibara, Baga, my former boy friend, and his age mate, Abube, approached and tried to take me away. At first they just coaxed me and teased. Abube was very helpful to Baga and wanted me to come with them, but Ohi was insistent that I stay with her. Baga was very angry and wanted to fetch his bow and arrows, but Abube stopped him. I was quite frightened by this and wanted to hurry on. I knew I could not get away even though I wanted to. I still liked Baga and wanted to marry him but I knew I had to go to Anona. I wanted to go right away and leave Baga now when he was so angry.

As we walked along the footpath, Ohi and I stood side by side. She was between me and the two men. We walked with our legs in unison, as if we were one person, so the men could not see that we were two people and shoot at us. But they did not do anything to us that day. However, Baga really wanted to marry me and not let me be married to Titio, and he did try to get me away.

Several months later Baga met me once and tried to grab me and take me away. We struggled but before long Titio's mother came and helped me. Another time I was working in my garden and Baga came to get me. He grabbed me but I screamed and someone working in a garden nearby heard me. She ran over to my garden and when Baga saw her he let go of me and ran away. Baga not only tried to take me away but he and Titio had several fights over me. I remember three different times Titio and Baga fought with each other over me. Baga really wanted to marry me and he was very angry that I had been given to Titio.

Baga was a stubborn man and he didn't give up easily. One time near Haparira the two men had a big fight. Not only the two of them but a lot of their friends were in it. Arrows came down just like rain. Both Titio and Baga were hurt; it was almost as if they had died. Both were hurt badly. I was right in the middle of it. Both of them were trying to get me and I was caught right in the middle.

After I went to Anona to live I was given some land on which to make a garden. I made a garden, worked hard in it, and after a while the food ripened. While the plants were growing Titio and I didn't have very much to do with each other. We were very much ashamed to be with each other, to see each other, or to talk to each other. I lived with his family but I would go back to my own village from time to time.

The garden grew and grew. Finally some food was ripe. It was time to consummate the marriage. There was a big feast at this time and I was to give him food that I had raised and cooked; then I would really be his wife. While most of the people were outside, Titio, his sister, Aantano, and I were in the house. She and I sat on one side of the hearth, Titio on the other. Aantano acted as interpreter for I didn't know much Agarabi and Titio didn't know much Tairora. I was very embarrassed at the time. I hung my head, twisted the cords on my skirt, and just sat there without anything to say.

I still didn't like this man. He was old and I was young. I did not want to be his wife. I was very unhappy during this whole time because I really didn't want to marry him. I was still trying to think of a way to get out of it. The food that I was supposed to give to Titio at this time was in my net bag. Aantano told me that Titio was asking for the food but I would not take it out of my net bag. Several times she told me that he was asking for the food but I did not want to give it to him. At first I was so embarrassed that I couldn't answer her. I couldn't say anything. I just sat there looking at the ground. I sat thinking about what I should do. What could I do? I really didn't want to give the food to him.

Finally, after Aantano had asked me again and again to talk, I told her that the food was in my net bag if the man wanted it. I was thinking about what I could do to get out of this but I did not think very well. I could think of nothing to do but I didn't want to give food to this man and become his wife. I had waited a long time to give him the food. My skirts, the new ones I got at my marriage, were no longer new. I had waited a long time. It was the fashion in those days to wait a long time, but I had waited very long.

Today the girls and boys do not wait long after the marriage. The girl gives food to the boy quickly so they can sleep together as man and wife. But when I was young we waited a long time. During this time Titio continued to cuddle with other girls although he and I could not cuddle with each other nor did we screw. I never did screw Titio because soon after I had given him the food he got sick and then he died.

I told you that I had not yet menstruated at the time of my marriage but it did happen later on. I was at Abiera at the time I first noticed the blood. I went to my mother's house and told her. Then she told some other women. Then a lot of my young girl friends came to the house to stay with me. My mother put some banana leaves and breadfruit leaves on the floor for me to sit on. They were changed once in a while. That is, new ones were brought in to replace the old ones, which were thrown away. Not only would this keep the blood from getting on the floor but also they would know when the blood had stopped and when it was time to have the feast. Mother tore the soiled leaves and threw them in the creek. They were carried away by the water so a sorcerer could not get them and work black magic on me.

There were quite a few girls with me. We talked, laughed, and joked a lot. We were brought food by my parents and other relatives as well as by the parents of the other girls. We girls didn't have to do any work at this time. We just stayed in the house and had a good time. When I had to piss or shit I could go outside, but that was the only time I could go out. I would put a bark blanket over my head and around my shoulders and go out. Two or three of the girls would go with me while I did this but I hid my face from anyone else. I was very embarrassed.

While we were in the house we had a lot of food and it was good. The food I ate was special food. My father or a father of the girls or one of our brothers would chew some wild ginger, pandanus nuts, a condiment, and aromatic bark, and then spit the mixture on the food before we ate it. While we were confined to the house we had a lot of food, food of all kinds, sweet potatoes, taro, yams, edible pitpit, sugar cane, bananas, greens, all kinds of food and it was good and there was a lot of it. Sometimes a woman or two would be in the house with us but often we were left alone.

Twice during the time of my first menstruation, groups of men would burst into the house and start to hit us girls. They would hit us with sticks, reeds, sugar cane, hit us on the head, arms, body, anywhere. The men would sometimes pick up a burning stick from the fire and burn us. Beho still has a scar. My father, my brothers, and my uncles wouldn't do this to me, but to others, and other girls' fathers and brothers did it to me. The men thought that all young girls are bigheads and they have to be punished and taught to forget about these bigheaded ways and grow up to be women who are not troublemakers. The men always think that young girls are too bigheaded for their own good. The men think the girls should not be bigheads and if they beat them and hit them, if they scare them, then the girls will not be bigheads and know-it-alls. They will behave themselves properly.

After the flow of blood had ceased it was time to have the feast. A lot of food had been brought to our village from the gardens. There was a great deal of food, high piles of food which had been brought in because it was going to be a big feast. A lot of pigs were killed too. We girls did not help, for we were still in the house getting dressed up for the feast. They put a lot of fresh pig grease on my skin and hair, I put my nose plugs in my nose—a piece of reed in the hole in my nasal septum and the bone of a fruit bat wing in the tip of my nose. Later Mando gave me a white stone to put in my nose hole but first I used only a reed. At the time of first menstruation a girl usually gets new skirts but I didn't because I still had some fairly new ones from my marriage and I wore these. I did get a new bark belt. A girl gets a new bark belt at this time and from then on she must always wear it except when she is pregnant and the belt gets too tight, or when she is an old woman. Then she can take it off if she wants to. I put red and green dracaena leaves in my armbands and I wore shell beads. I was all dressed up.

Then all of us girls walked out of the house to the place where the feast was being held. We went out together in a line. Then we sat down. We were brought food and we ate it. We were served the first food, then the other people were served. Everyone but the unmarried older boys could eat. They could not eat food at the feast of the first menses. My mother's relatives were given a lot of food at this time.

At the time of first menstruation I went to my mother's house; that was the fashion before. After that when I was menstruating I went to the menstrual hut and stayed there during the period, for it was dangerous to let the blood get around. Today most women do not go to the menstrual hut. In the villages it is still considered dangerous for a man to eat food that has been cooked by a woman who is menstruating, so at this time a man gets his food from his mother or sister or some other woman. After cessation of the menses a woman will cook some food and give it to her husband to tell him that her period has finished. Husband and wife would be very embarrassed to talk about this to each other.

So, I never slept with my husband. After he had eaten the food I gave him he was working in one of his gardens when he began to feel ill. Titio reported that a sorcerer had appeared. Titio stared at him, looked at him directly and piercingly. Then Titio's head began to ache. I had gone to collect firewood, and as I was coming back Ohira called to me and told me that Titio was ill. I dropped the wood and went to see him. He was awake but he was in great pain and a number of people had already gathered around him as he lay on the ground. Some of the men took him to the men's house. They helped him as he tried to walk although he stumbled a great deal. He stayed in the men's house for four nights and then, because he was not getting any better, they took him to his mother's village. It was there he died.

Many people came to mourn for him and to see him buried but I did not stay for that. The day after Titio died, Ubaio died at Bahiora and I came back to mourn her and to see her buried. Many people were angry with me because I did not stay at Titio's village until after he was buried, but Ubaio died and I wanted to come back here. I still did not like Titio or want to be married to him. I don't know who worked the black magic against Titio and made him die. A while after his death, Ajto, his stepfather, determined who had done it. He made several packets of small pieces of sweet potatoes, greens, and pig liver, wrapped in dracaena leaves. Each package was given the name of a village where the guilty sorcerer might be living. The packages were cooked in an earth oven, and after they were taken out they were examined. The one that was not completely cooked indicated the location of the culprit. The spirit of the sorcerer was stuck to the food which prevented it from cooking properly and thus Ajto knew who had done it. However, I don't know who it was. Ajto never told me and I never asked him about it.

I was not sorry when Titio died. I don't know how Baho felt about his death. She was also betrothed to Titio. She was to marry him after I did, but he died before she had been sent to him. I don't think she was very sorry, but I don't know. Later she went into Kainantu to live with a White man and then after he divorced her and left, she came back to Haparira and married Bebo and she still is with him. I really don't know how she felt about Titio, but I don't think she liked him very well. I don't think she was sorry when he died although he would have been her husband.

Even though I didn't like Titio he was my husband, so when he died one of my finger joints was cut off. It was our custom to cut a finger joint of a woman when her husband, father, or brother died. Some old women had few fingers left on their hands. Also, before the White man came and brought metal tools, finger joints were cut off with stone adzes. Mine was cut off with a machete. I held the finger on a stone, with the other fingers curled under so they wouldn't be injured. Then Bai cut if off and threw it away. I didn't watch her while she did it. I looked the other way. It hurt because she had to cut several times; she was not strong enough to chop it off with one blow as is usually done. She just threw the finger in the creek.

After Titio died I put on some mourning clothes but I did not go through mourning as if I had been married a long time. A woman usually cut her husband's net bag and bark blanket into strips, put them on and wore them. She would hang his belt around her shoulder. If he chewed betel, she wore his lime stick and sometimes his lime gourd suspended from her neck or shoulder. She also wore a piece of his hair in a little pouch suspended from a cord around her neck. Many women still do these things although they usually just tear up a laplap instead of a bark blanket. In my mourning for Titio I wore only his net bag and his belt. I didn't have any of his hair in a pouch.

I observed some of the food taboos. I didn't eat yams, sugar cane, taro, or some kinds of bananas, nor did I drink water from certain streams. But I didn't stop doing these things for very long and I didn't stop eating all the things older women do. I continued to eat pig when it was available. I didn't eat sweet potato for two or three days. When I could eat it again Ajto chewed some gingerroot, tree bark, and a condiment and spit this mixture onto the sweet potatoes which I ate for the first time. After that I could eat as many as I wanted to. Because I was widowed so young I stayed in mourning but a short time. Women usually mourned for a long time. After a woman was through with mourning, all of her old clothes and all of her husband's things were burned. They were rubbed with pig grease and pig blood and then burned. The widow, who had not washed or braided her hair during the period of mourning, had it cut with a bamboo knife, covered with fresh pig grease, and braided again.

The mourning period for a woman is usually much longer than it is for a man because men can't get along as well without a wife as women can get along without a husband. After the mourning period is over, a woman can marry again. One of her husband's brothers has first choice if he wants to marry her but this is not always the case. If another man wanted to marry her he could let her know by giving her a banana leaf and a piece of banana root. If she accepted them, the two would go to a stream and throw the leaf and root into the water. Now it is different. A man who wants to marry a widow goes to her house and offers her a cigarette. If she accepts the cigarette, she accepts his proposal. Some women are not anxious to remarry and they will refuse a number of offers. Some of them are so bad about turning suitors away that their brothers get cross with them and argue with them. A man wants his sister to marry again but she might not want to.

The first time a girl is married she may be given to a boy whose sister was given to her brother. When this happens, less pay is given to the girl's family. But this doesn't always happen and then a lot of pay must be given. Sometimes a boy doesn't have to give pay at all even if he has not given his sister to the girl's brother. He can pull the girl away from her family to himself by a ceremony we call *hampu*. He and his brothers and friends go to a hillside, dig a large hole, have a large fire and sing and sing and sing. The girl will hear this, even if her village is quite far away. She will be overpowered by the singing and want to run away and marry the boy. This does not happen often, but when it does the girl remembers it and is always talking about it. She likes to talk about it, to tell her children and her grandchildren. This kind of elopement is not common but when it happens the boy doesn't have to give any pay to the girl's family. Opu attracted Najna in this way and I think that Gahabu's mother was enticed by *hampu*. I don't know of very many women that were pulled in this way, but there is always a lot of talk about it when it happens.

There are some ways of marrying that are not right. Some of them are very bad but they sometimes happen. Akro's marriage with Aru, his third wife, is not right. He used to have three wives but he divorced the first two and now just has Aru. You remember when you were here in 1954, Akro had two wives. They both lived at Tonkei and Akro would come out to the village often. He worked in Kainantu but he would also come out to the village to be with his wives. But he wanted a wife to live in Kainantu so in 1955 he married Aru and she has lived in Kainantu since then.

But their marriage is not right. That is because they were kin of each other before they were married. Akro called Aru "sister's daughter" and Aru called Akro "mother's brother." It is very wrong for two people in that relationship to marry each other. But Akro and Aru did it and nothing has happened to them. Aru hasn't had any children but I don't think it is because of her improper marriage. I think she has eaten some "medicine" to keep her from having children. But the marriage was not right; it is as if Akro ate dog shit.

To Kainantu and Motherhood

AFTER TITIO DIED I CONTINUED TO LIVE WITH HIS PARENTS at Anona. One day Titio's younger sister and I went out to the garden to get some sweet potatoes. Most of the people had left the village to collect grass for a police sergeant in Kainantu who was building a house. A lot of the Anona people were getting thatch for him. He had asked the Kainoas to bring reeds, the Kamano to bring bamboo, the Anonas to bring thatch.

We went to the garden. After we came back she said, "Let's leave the worst sweet potatoes here in the village for feeding the pigs and take the best to our friends in Kainantu." I said, "No. I don't think we should do that." I knew everyone would be angry with us. But Ampiso said it didn't matter, that we should go. She was insistent and I gave in. We started out and after we crossed the Ramu River we crept along in the tall grass on the west side of the road so we wouldn't be seen.

After we got rid of the sweet potatoes we went to Pona's house. I didn't want to go there but Ampiso was insistent. Pona, from Abiera, is now married to Ioga. When she was about sixteen years old she was to have married Koraw, a boy at Ehubajra for whom she had been indicated. He was a very young boy and she didn't want to marry such a young boy. So she ran away to Anona, where her mother's family lived, and later she married Nabari, a boy from the Sepik district on the coast, a close friend of Robaga. Nabari worked for the government and he and Pona lived in the building with other married New Guinean employees of the government. Nabari later divorced Pona and left Kainantu. She then returned to her village to live and she married Ioga.

When Ampiso and I went to Pona's house that time I was still wearing my mourning dress: Titio's belt over my shoulder, a few strips of cloth hanging from my skirt, and two strips hanging from the net cap that I still wore on my head. Many times Ampiso had tried to talk me into going into Kainantu to live. I was still very frightened of Kainantu. I was afraid of all the people at the government station. I thought they were spirit men of some kind.

Ampiso told me to take off my mourning clothes and she would give them to her mother, my mother-in-law. I thought about it. Ampiso kept after me about it. She said, "You are really wild. Men and women are talking about you. They think you are a spirit woman and they are saying bad things about you. You should hide. But you are a young woman, you are too young to go hide and stay with the natives who think you are a spirit woman." Ampiso used to talk this way to me, so finally I gave in, took off my mourning decorations, and gave them to Ampiso and went to Kainantu to live with Pona and her husband.

After I had been with them a while Nabari told me that the *kiap* would probably be asking why I was staying in Kainantu and that if I didn't want the *kiap* to send me away I'd better tell him I had come there to marry someone. Nabari suggested that I marry Robaga, a friend and companion of his from the coast, a man I didn't know. I hadn't met him yet. Robaga had been married before, to a Kamano woman who didn't take good care of him. She didn't cook for him and they didn't have any children. The *kiap* didn't want unattached females around because he suspected them of being whores. Eventually the *kiap* called me in and asked me what I was doing in Kainantu and I told him that I had come to marry Robaga, the cook for the doctor. So he let me stay.

A while later, still before I married Robaga, Nabari, Pona, and I went to Aiyura. We slept there on Saturday and Sunday and then started back to Kainantu. There were a lot of soldiers on the road that day and many of them were looking for girls they could fuck. Some of them tried to make advances to Pona and me. Even though Pona's husband was with her, a couple of the soldiers tried to get her away. They tried to get Nabari to let them sleep with us and they offered to pay him for it.

Pona and I were very frightened. We stayed close to Nabari at first and then we got so scared that we ran to a nearby village for protection. When Robaga heard about this he sent his cook to get me and take me back to Kainantu. I still did not go to live with Robaga. I didn't really want to do it, although because I had told the *kiap* I was going to marry him I felt that I had to do it if I wanted to remain in Kainantu. Robaga sent a blanket to me.

It was about then that my hair was cut short for the first time. The native women at the Seventh Day Adventist mission station shaved my hair for the first time. They used a razor and it pulled my hair. It hurt and it felt cold for quite a while afterward. I didn't like it and I would often think how nice it would be when I could go back to being a villager again and braid my hair and let it hang down to my shoulders. I thought then that probably Robaga would leave Kainantu some day and that he would divorce me and I could return to the village and braid my hair again. I also got cotton clothes for the first time now. The doctor gave some clothes to Robaga and told him they were for his wife. A Seventh Day Adventist woman sewed the wraparound skirt for me and there was a long overblouse to go with it.

Titio's parents and relatives did not want me to marry Robaga. They were angry about it and they took the case to court in Kainantu. Panke went with me when I first went to court. There was a lot of talk and then the *kiap* told me to go get my father, that my father must come to court to help me. I thought he meant Mando but a policeman told me, "No, he means your real father, he means Bano, he is your real father, not Mando."

So I came out here to the village. I was wearing a dress that day, one of the long white, Mother Hubbard dresses that the mission first wanted native women to wear. When I saw him I called out to Bano and he became frightened when he saw someone who was wearing clothes. He didn't look closely and he didn't know who it was but thought that maybe it was a policeman or the *kiap*. He was still a fugitive, for he'd not been caught after he broke out of jail. He was afraid of meeting someone who might know about that and send him back to jail. I shouted who I was and finally he stopped and we talked. I asked him if he would go to court with me. He said that because of his illegal status he couldn't go to Kainantu with me. He said that I should have Mando do it because Mando had been acting as my father since my mother died.

So I got Mando and he went into Kainantu with me. After everyone did a lot of talking and arguing the *kiap* decided that I was free to marry Robaga. Titio's father had not given all the pay for me that he should have, so I did not have to stay with him or marry someone he wanted me to marry. I was free to marry Robaga. Robaga made payments to my relatives for me. He gave three knives, two steel axes, and two small strings of shell. Mando and Bano each kept an axe and a knife. Beja kept a knife. The shells were distributed to a lot of relatives. Robaga gave good pay for me but there was no feast.

At the time I went to Robaga he lived near the doctor's house, which was near the infirmary then located near the Seventh Day Adventist mission. The doctor did not stay in Kainantu much but made trips to the villages in the area and Robaga would go with him to cook for him. I would stay in Kainantu while they were away.

The doctor was not married but would sleep with various local women. Robaga and I lived in a thatch house near the doctor's house. I did not know how to speak Pidgin but I learned it fairly quickly, and after I had learned it both the doctor and the *kiap* would use me as an interpreter. They didn't pay me for it though. There was still no money here; pay would be in the form of steel axes, knives, clothes, salt, and things like that.

Mando approved of my going to Kainantu to live. He encouraged me to stay there, to learn to talk Pidgin and to become "our interpreter." I was a bit shy at first in the new surroundings. The food was very different from any I had known and I did not like some of it. I liked rice, porridge, and fresh beef all right, but I thought that corned beef tasted like the skin of a dead man. I liked pumpkin and corn, although it was the first time I had eaten them. I thought wheat flour and scones were awful! I didn't eat very much at first because even the things that weren't too bad I didn't really like very much. I did have a garden of my own in which I grew sweet potatoes and other things but I didn't have any yams or taro. Several times I would pick things from the Seventh Day Adventist gardens, but Robaga told me I shouldn't do that since their gardens didn't belong to us. I had to learn how to cook, too, because at first I didn't know anything about cooking these new foods. Robaga taught me how to cook and finally I learned how to do it. I even got so I could go to collect our rations every fortnight. These included rice, canned meat, tobacco, and salt.

When I first lived in Kainantu, that was in 1943, it was a much smaller place than it is today. The Seventh Day Adventist station had two metal-roofed houses, one for living and one for storage. The latrine was still made of thatch. The *kiap* lived in the old house facing the government storehouse. It was metal roofed and was the only *kiap* house there was then. The government office was located near where it is now but it had plank walls and a thatch roof and was raised only slightly off the ground, not high as it is today. To the east of it was the government storehouse made of thatch. There were no bicycles then, no motorbikes or cars except one Jeep that belonged to the government. After the miners had sent a lot of gold out of here things began to pick up and better and more buildings were built.

But when I first went to live in Kainantu there was not much there. The doctor lived in a grass house near the Seventh Day Adventist station and the infirmary was there too. In 1946 the infirmary was moved to a thatch house near the Tapo road and in 1948 it was moved to its present location. The first buildings were still thatch roofed. One night the doctor's house burned and after that the first metal roofed house was built for the doctor. It was the one you stayed in in 1954. A year before you came that time the second doctor's house was built.

In 1943 the houses of the married employees of the government were located where the tennis courts are now just west of the office. The police house and the jail were east of the office down near where the road turns to go to the trade store. The old airstrip was near the agricultural agent's to the west of the road as it leaves the present airstrip going to Aiyura. This airstrip was built in 1944–45.

In 1953 the houses of married employees were moved south of the airstrip and in 1954 the jail was moved to the south side of the airstrip. The early stores were built in 1950 and 1951. In 1943, too, horses were kept near the old airstrip. The government used horses quite a bit in those days. The oldest metal roofed house in the area is Mata Johannes's at Raipinka. It was built when he came back after World War II, and when he first built the Lutheran mission at Raipinka.

All during this time I did not go back to Abiera to visit very often. One time though when I was walking back to Kainantu from there I remember that I met a ghost. Along the big road, near where it crosses the Ramu River, I saw a man with a net bag and there were shillings in the net bag. He was holding his hands on his head. I said to Gau, the boy who was walking with me, "See that man over there." "What man? There is no man there." "Over there, he's standing right by the tall grass. See him?" "No, there's no one there."

But I still saw him. I was frightened, so Gau and I went into a house to cook some food and I thought the man would go away. Gau still could not see him. But I had seen him and then he followed us for a while. We went into a house and a woman was there. She gave us some food, some cooked sweet potatoes. I couldn't eat very much because I was so nervous about the man who had followed us.

I left some of my food by the fire when we went to sleep. During the night, the man came into the house and ate the food I had left by the fire. He ate very fast, like this [she demonstrates]. I watched him and after a while I saw him go outside. When dawn came Gau woke up and was hungry and wanted to eat the food that I had left by the fire. I told him that he couldn't because the man had come and eaten it and it was gone.

But Gau said, "No, the food is there, let me eat it." I looked and, true, the food was there. It was a spirit that I had seen, the spirit of some man. I told Gau not to eat the food because a spirit had been around it and touched it and eaten some of it and it might make him sick. I don't know whose spirit it was.

Even after money was introduced there was not much of it. In Kainantu not many people had money. Most pay continued to be made with steel axes, knives, cloth, beads, and things like that. There was some money though. There were some small coins. Robaga would keep what money he had in a worn-out stocking of the doctor's that he kept in the bedroom. We put all the money we could in the stocking.

One time I wanted to buy something and I told Robaga that I wanted some money. He went to get it but there was no money in the stocking. Where had it gone? We were both very surprised. We talked about what could have happened to it? Who would steal it? We wondered about its disappearing. I wanted Robaga to go and tell the Doctor what had happened but Robaga didn't want to do it. I said he should go tell the Master, but he was insistent, he didn't want to. Later he admitted that he had lied to me, had taken the money to play Lucky, and had lost it in the card game and had not told me about it. When I wanted some money he lied and said it had been stolen. But really he had taken it and lost it gambling. I did not get cross with him because most of the time he was good to me.

There was not much money at first and when I got some I would save it to buy things. But some of it I would give to Mando when I went back to Abiera. The first coins that I gave him were the kind without holes in them. He took a nail and pounded it with a stone to make holes in the coins. Then he strung them and wore them for decoration. This was the first money he had had and he thought it was for ornamentation.

With the first money I had to spend I bought a string of bright colored beads for three shillings. Other things that I got with some of the first money I had were a laplap for seven shillings and two machetes for seven shillings each. I did not get these all at one time, for I did not have that much money. I got the beads first and when I had saved enough money I got the other things. We had mostly small coins—pennies, threepence, sixpence, and a few shillings. There were not many stores. The one where I bought my things was near Raipinka. It was there that I bought the beads and other things.

I used to try to get Bano to go into Kainantu to talk to the *kiap* and get things straightened out with him. I told him it was no good not to. Since he broke out of jail his name had not been on the government books, and the policemen could always catch him and take him back to jail. I told Bano that the No good time was over. The time when the *kiap*s shot and killed people and herded them like animals was all over and he should go in and get things straightened out with the government. I said I didn't think he would be punished. Finally Bano did go into Kainantu to talk to the *kiap* and there was no trouble at all. This *kiap* did not know about Bano's jailbreak nor even about Bano. So when Bano came in he had his name put on the book again and nothing was said about his running away from jail. No one knew anything about it. So it was good that Bano came in and got things straightened out.

After I learned that Bano was my father, I remembered some of the things I knew about him when I thought he was just another man. Bano had five wives. The fourth wife was Tonkei. That old, almost blind man you saw at Koraw's feast last week, the old man from Bontaa, many years ago liked Tonkei even though she was married to Bano. He liked her and she liked him. One time he told her to meet him at a garden and they would screw. He wanted to fuck. When he asked her he gave her a piece of pig.

Bano learned about this. I don't know how he learned about it, but when the two lovers met, Bano was watching them. He watched them embrace and fondle each other. I don't know if they really started to fuck. I don't think so, but I really don't know. Bano ran out at them and started to fight. The man got away, he was hit, but not hurt badly and he ran away. Bano hit Tonkei with a stick, hit her and hit her, again and again. He really beat her up. She was a light-skinned woman but when he got through with her she was black all over, her skin was black. And she was bleeding in a lot of places. He hit her everywhere, all her bones, joints, all over.

When he finished, some of her bones were broken and she was very limp, only her liver wasn't broken. She couldn't hold her arms up, she was just limp. They carried her back to the village and she died that night. Her relatives didn't do anything about it because they said it was her fault for committing adultery. They didn't try to do anything to Bano.

Bano also killed another woman, a woman he wanted to marry. She had been married before. After her husband died, both Bano and his brother Bonabu wanted to marry her. She would have been Bano's sixth wife. There was a big fight and she was shot and killed by an arrow that Bano shot. They said Bano didn't mean to kill her but he killed her by accident while this big fight was going on.

After I was married to Robaga I did not go back to Abiera often, just occasionally. But when people from Abiera came into Kainantu they would come to see me and bring me news from the village. A while after I had been married to Robaga, I did not menstruate. I missed several times and then one day when I was talking to Ihoa, she said that I was going to have a baby and that as it was to be my first child I must come back to Abiera soon and they would make it all right.

I went to Abiera but Robaga didn't go with me. He never did go to Abiera very much. I would always go without him. I would walk with someone, but Robaga usually did not go with me—almost never at that early time. When I came back to Abiera that time they had a big feast and a lot of people came to it. My maternal relatives gave it although it wasn't their obligation to do it, but because I had married an outsider they wanted these things done and so they did it. Also, although I knew by now that Bano, not Mando, was my father, Mando continued to act like my real father on many occasions.

This time, then, my mother's brother gave the feast for the first time I was with child. They gathered a lot of food, all kinds of food, got it ready, and had a big feast. Lots of sweet potatoes, edible pitpit, greens, taro, yams, bananas, all kinds of food. Before the food had finished cooking, Mando took me out in front of everyone and I sat down on a banana leaf. Then Mando set up the banana stalk at which I was to shoot an arrow. He could use taro or banana. People used either one. But this time Mando cut a banana stalk and set it up. Then he gave me a bow and arrows to shoot at the banana stalk.

I stood up and I shot at the stalk, but I was not very good and I missed. Then I shot another arrow and it hit the banana trunk. Everyone knew then that I would have a baby boy. Mando's wife and Ihua then washed me. I sat down on the banana leaf. They put a bamboo tube on my bead. In it were rats, fruit bats, and greens. The rats and fruit bats had been caught earlier, then dried and stored in the roof of the house.

Mando poured water on the bamboo tube on my head and on my abdomen. Then Ihua and Taramao rubbed my stomach with the water that fell on it. They did this to "heat my belly." This was to make sure I would have a lot of children. This completed the ceremony and then the earth oven was opened and we ate. The food was divided among the guests but I don't remember just how. All I know is that there was a lot of it and everyone had plenty to eat as well as some to take home.

While we were eating, Ihua took the banana stalk that I shot down to the river. She put it in the water. She did not throw it in. She slid it in gently so my unborn child would not be hurt.

After this feast I returned to Kainantu and waited until it was almost time for the baby to be born. I then went back to Abiera. The doctor in Kainantu at that time did not deliver babies. He was just a patrol doctor who went around to villages to help sick people. There was not yet a big infirmary in Kainantu. Nor was there a proper childbirth hut in Kainantu for me to use.

So I went back to Abiera and to my relatives to have my first child. I came back here to Ikubakira, where Mando, Beja, Toagara, and some of the others then had their pig houses. It was at Ikubakira that my first baby was born, and it was a boy. I did not go to a childbirth house to have this baby. The people were living in their pig houses at the time and Paulo was born in one of the pig houses at Ikubakira.

Villages used to have small houses in a hidden spot at one side of the village where a woman would go to have her baby. She would not go alone, because it would be too dangerous. Her mothers or sisters would go with her to feed her and to help her when the baby came. Also, if an enemy came near they could get help. Sometimes a woman had to go alone. If the baby came quickly she would rush to the childbirth house. Or if a woman wanted to kill her baby she would go there alone.

But we were taught that it was not good to go there alone. They told us this story about it. A Tairora woman was beginning to have labor pains. She didn't feel good so she went to the childbirth house. She went alone. After the baby was born, she stayed there still alone. A Kamano man came. He thought it was an ordinary house. He came in. He lit a fire. He covered the child with a skirt. Just the woman was there. Her mother wasn't there. Her sister wasn't with her. She was alone.

The man got fire and put it outside the house. The woman said to the man "You come in here. You come inside." He came in. He had taken off his breech clout. The woman saw his genitals. Then they screwed. Then the man wanted to rest. The woman said, "You warm yourself by the fire. You rest."

Then the woman went outside. She left the childbirth house. She went back to the village. She called her husband. She called all the people. They came. She told them about what had happened. About the intercourse. All the men and women were angry. They all went to the childbirth hut.

The man was still there resting. They trapped him. Then they killed the man. They cut him up into tiny pieces. They cut his bones, his genitals, his head. They cut and cut all of him up into tiny pieces. Then they set fire to the childbirth house and he was burned with it.

We were always told another story too. One time long ago, all the men and women wanted to go to Ontabura for a dance. One woman was pregnant and she and her mother did not go with the others. They went to the childbirth house together. At the childbirth house the mother said, "You go cover the path. Go get some reeds and taboo the road." (If we don't want people to use a footpath or if we want them to go around something, like a banana tree we own, one with ripe fruit on it, this is what we do: we cover the path with some reeds or other plants or we can bend the leaves on a plant that is growing by the path. These are ways we can tell people not to use the path, not to use that part of the path. We call this "tabooing" the road.)

The two women were very frightened to be at the childbirth house alone. They put cane leaves across the road to camouflage it. The woman had her baby. The two women stayed in the childbirth house.

After a while a man came along the path. He saw the reeds. He moved the reeds. He crept nearer and nearer to the childbirth house. He saw the smoke from the fire which the two women had inside. The man got a piece of reed and he imitated the sound of a pig so the women would not know a man was nearby. But they knew. The mother said, "You have given birth to a baby. Your husband is outside coming to see it. He sees the reeds now."

She said it loud so the man could hear. The baby's mother handed the baby to her mother. The women had a small fire made of sticks. They pretended to be asleep. The man thought they were asleep. The grandmother held the baby.

The baby's mother was lying on her back. Her legs were spread apart. Between them she held a stone adze. She held it very tightly. The man came in. He put his head down to the fire and blew on it. The woman hit him on the back of the head with the stone adze. She cut his head off. The head stayed inside the house. The women threw the body outside. The two women went to sleep. At dawn they got up. They put on their best finery and decorations. They put red coloring on their skin and they put black paint on their skin. The baby's mother handed it to her mother. She put on a grass skirt. She shouted loudly. She shouted, "Fire! Fire!"

All the men and women who had gone to Ontabura looked

Anyan and baby daughter in 1964.

Carrying pandanus mats, firewood,
and net bags filled with sweet potatoes,
unmarried girls return to the village
from their gardens.

An elder supervises her adolescent granddaughter
as she rolls bark fibers together along her thigh
to make a strong cord with multiple uses.

Above: Two visitors from Kainantu spend
the afternoon with friends in the village.

Top left: Using a bone needle threaded with fiber cord,
a woman sews pandanus leaves together to make a mat
used variously from sleeping pad to rain gear.

Bottom left: Holding a bundle of thatch in her left hand,
a worker takes time out from roof repair for a "smoke."
Note the headbands, necklace of dog teeth and shell,
woven arm bands, and the net bag covering her head.

The ubiquitous net bag, worn tumpline fashion by females,
is hung to one side to display ceremonial cicatrizes.
Note the two-strand "belt" above her skirt
worn by all non-pregnant females of childbearing age.

The *longabura,* a one-stringed bow instrument,
produces soft, rather monotonous sounds.

A birthing/menstrual hut no longer in use
and falling into decay.

back. They saw the women. They said, "Who is it that we have left back at the village? There are two women there." Then they went back to the village. They saw the man who had been killed. He was an enemy. They were very glad the woman killed him. They told the woman she did a good thing to kill the man. They told her that she looked after things very well while everyone was away. They were very pleased with her.

A few days after my baby was born, I don't remember how many, there was a feast. We always have a feast for a new-born child. It is very important for a first-born child especially if it is a boy. Most people would rather have boys than girls, and the father makes a big feast if his wife has a baby boy. But Robaga was not here, he didn't belong to Tairora anyway and didn't know about our customs, so Mando gave the feast for the new baby.

It was a big feast but not as big as if we had been at the village rather than at the pig houses or if the baby's father were present. Robaga named the baby Paulo, named him after a friend of his from the coast. Mando and Bano each gave him a name too. For a while my father's relatives used the name that Bano had given him and my mother's relatives used the name that Mando had given him.

Although most people called him Paulo, when he comes out here to Abiera some of the older people still use his other names. Everyone in Kainantu calls him Paulo. Mando gave the feast this time and the food that was given away went to Marabeba, Nagary, and Bano, and they divided it among their relatives. At the feast for a child the father of the child eats some half-cooked taro and his brothers usually eat this with him. But Robaga did not do that.

After a while I took Paulo to Kainantu. Robaga was anxious to have me come back there; he did not want me to stay at Abiera too long because he was afraid I might still want to be a village woman and leave him for a Tairora man. I did not have a new net bag for Paulo but just an old one in which I carried him back to Kainantu. I put some banana leaves in the bottom of it, then layers of other leaves and soft bark on that and put him on top. I didn't have any pieces of cloth for him then. Paulo was born in January of 1946 and he is my oldest child.

After Paulo's umbilical cord fell off I wrapped it in some leaves and gave it to Aroba when I saw him. I knew he would take care of it. I knew that some time he would go up on one of the mountains above Abiera and shoot the cord away. He would tie the cord to an arrow and then shoot it upward with his bow. That is what was done with the cords of babies after they dropped off. Sometimes it was done immediately or sometimes one waited quite a while to do it. Aroba did this with the cords of four others of my children and either he or Ika will do it for Wanama. I still have her cord in this little knit bag that I got from the Salvation Army Sisters at Kainantu. It contained medicine when I got it. Later I will give it to either Aroba or Ika and he will shoot the cord up the mountain.

Another ceremony that was held for Paulo at Abiera was at the time he was "washed." This is done by the mother's relatives. Ika made a small saucer-shaped depression in the ground. He lined it with banana leaves and then put Paulo on them. Then all of my brothers and sisters took turns at "washing" him. They each put some water on him. Haru took the baby and then gave it to Hinda or Ampe, I don't remember which one. They all did it one after another. Then the baby was dried and offered to me. I was sitting nearby with my legs and arms bent.

I held out my hands for the baby and then when Ampe was going to give it to me she pulled it back and said, "This doesn't belong to you, it belongs to me." Again I held out my hands as she offered the baby. But just as it came near my hands she pulled it back again and said it was hers. It didn't belong to me. This happened several times. This is the way it is usually done. Finally, she gave it to me. If all the aunts and uncles don't wash the child it will get sick. By having this washing it means that the mother's relatives accept the child and their particular relationship to it. Paulo is the only one of my children who had this done, this "wash wash" by my relatives.

Paulo is also the only child of mine that was born in the village. My second child, Yebi, was born in Kainantu in 1948. She was born in Kainantu and was named by Robaga although Mando and Bano also gave her names. The feast for Yebi was also held in Kainantu. Robaga gave away some things but my relatives from Abiera also brought a lot of food for the feast.

Before this though, but after Paulo was born, a sister of mine, an older sister, Tera, died. I came back to the village and stayed here two nights until after they buried her. Tera had two children. The first one died when it was very young, still in the net bag. The second one died when it was still in her womb, and she died at the same time. I went back to Abiera for the burial.

The day after Tera was buried I went to a garden down by the Ramu River to get beans. Karehu was with me. When we came back up on the road we met Bano and he told us about the spirits that hang around Kambuta and Bahiora. Ghosts of all the people—relatives, brothers and sisters, who had died earlier. He talked about them and then told us that when I was born one of them had taken my good legs and given me legs that were not very good. The legs I now have are not very good and I cannot walk fast; I always walk slowly. Bano said that I was not a woman who could walk around fast but one who must go slowly because the ghosts had buggered up my legs. He said that I must get going on my way back to Kainantu. That I shouldn't stop and rest. Also that I shouldn't get to Kainantu late so the *kiap* would be angry with me for being on the road late at night.

I believed him and I started on my way. But when I got to where Borawta is now, I "heard" his admonition again. By five o'clock I was at Ontabura. By six o'clock I was at Buntera, this side of Haparira. I wasn't frightened. I was alone, all alone, but I wasn't frightened at all. I wasn't afraid of anything. I walked and walked, all alone. But I didn't get scared. My spirit was not afraid. I walked and walked. Then I came to a house that had a big fire inside. It was a small house and a lot of smoke was coming out of it. I wondered who was inside. I wondered if I could sleep in this house. But there was no one there, only smoke, and so I thought I shouldn't stop.

I put my ear up to the house wall but didn't hear anyone; just the smoke was coming out of the house. There wasn't anyone there. I didn't hear any men or women talking, no one was there. I walked along the fence and I hit my leg on a stone and it hurt. It didn't hurt much, just a little bit. It did bleed but I didn't really feel much.

Then my spirit came to a house and I saw a lot of men and women and they were singing and dancing. They came near the fence and they were singing and dancing. A lot of men and women were there now. I went quite near them but not enough really to see them well. But there were a lot of men and women and they were all singing and dancing near the fence but I didn't recognize them. The necks of the women were different from ours. I heard the singing but I didn't see well at all who it was.

It was very dark by now and the path was not good but my legs just kept on going. I couldn't see the path, it was too dark for that, pitch black, but my legs just kept walking on and on. I came up the mountain beyond Haparira and I heard a bird call out. I looked and tried to see the bird but I couldn't see it. It was on the ground. I looked until my eyes hurt. I stood up and looked and looked but I could not see the bird.

When it was beginning to get light I came up to the bridge near McBeath's store. I heard singing again. It was in my language. I thought, "What is it that I hear?" At ten o'clock I came to Kainantu to the *kiap*'s. I went there and stood up. The police sergeant looked at me. He just looked and looked. He was holding a bow and arrows. He asked me why I had been walking alone at night. "Why did you come back to Kainantu in the middle of the night?" I said, "I have just come, that's all."

What had happened was that my father had talked to the ghosts and the ghosts brought me to Kainantu. I tire easily when I walk but my legs don't hurt. It wasn't a bird I heard, it was the ghost, that's all.

One night in Kainantu, later on, when it was near the time for me to have my third child, I was going to the mission for a lesson. It was about seven o'clock in the evening and Paulo and Yebi were with me. I was wearing a raincoat and carrying a lamp. As we passed the stream on the way to the mission I saw a man in the water. He wanted the coat and he tried to take it from me. He even spit at me. The man talked and talked—or that is what I thought, but really it was a spirit who was taking my unborn child. The man talked and talked, and his talk was like that of a spirit I had seen once before on the road. The man talked to my two children. He talked to the big child and the little child.

That night I dreamt about two children, one big and one little. The next day around noon I began to feel the pains. In the evening I had my third child in the childbirth house at Kainantu. But the cord was not properly tied and the child bled to death. All his blood left him. It was the ghost that made him die. I think that it was the ghost of my first husband that did it. This baby was not named.

When Paulo and Yebi were small I didn't make them stop sucking at the breast until I had to. Paulo couldn't do much after Yebi was born, although I would let him suck sometimes after she had eaten. I had to keep him from doing it as much as he wanted, because Yebi had to have plenty of milk. But I had a lot of milk and sometimes Paulo could have some.

Because my third baby died when it was born Yebi could continue to suckle for a long time. She suckled at my breasts longer than Paulo did. She continued until my fourth child was born and she was quite big by then. I didn't put anything on my breasts to make the children stop sucking in those days. Just let them continue as long as they needed the milk. Some women who get tired of nursing rub some leaves with a bitter taste on their breasts so the baby will not like it.

But with my last four children, I have tried to stop them from sucking. I took some leaves from a plant that has a bitter juice. Then I crushed them and rubbed them on my breasts so the juice covered them. The doctor at the infirmary tells us that it is all right to do this after a baby has four teeth. Wanama's teeth are very sharp now. She still wants to suck my breast even when there is no milk. Even during the night when she is sleeping next to me she will sometimes suck. You see other women whose breasts hurt when they are scratched by a child's sucking. And you remember the woman that came in from the bush with an infected breast. Her child had cut her. Her little boy had cut her with his teeth.

When a baby's teeth are coming in, sometimes they hurt quite a bit. Some children hurt more than others. They like to chew on things or sometimes we rub their gums with our fingers. Some mothers put leaf juice on their fingers when they rub the gums. But not all do. One thing we can do is to give the child a betel nut to chew on. That is hard and soothes the child. But many children still like to suck. Wanama is one, and the last time we were in Kainantu the doctor gave her a pacifier. She wears it on a string around her neck. But as you know, she does not suck it. She just chews on the plastic ring.

In those times too we didn't start to give the babies other kinds of food as early as many mothers in Kainantu do now. I don't remember just when I gave solid foods to my eldest children. But sometimes I would chew up a bit of sweet potato or taro, chew it very well and then take some in my fingers and put it in the baby's mouth. I didn't force them to eat it. I would give them little bits of food just to taste, when they were small. With my last three or four children I did not chew the food I first gave to them. I mashed the vegetables with a fork. Then I gave it to the baby with a spoon. Or sometimes I would make a thick soup of sweet potatoes or yams and feed them that on a spoon. For all of my children it was a long time before I gave them very much of it. They could have a lot of milk for as long as they liked it. I had a lot of milk with my children. We were always good to our children and let them suck when they wanted to. Even when we were working in the garden we would stop work when they cried and let them suck.

Sometimes if the child was not a tiny baby and didn't really need the milk but just wanted to suck, and if we were busy, we'd let some other woman do it. Some other woman, even an old woman, would help us take care of a child. If the child became fussy this other woman would let the child suck her nipple. This was very common. If the child was a very young child who was really hungry, this wouldn't help much. The child would still continue to cry because it was hungry. But an older child who wasn't very hungry but just wanted to suck would be satisfied to suck this old dry teat. When babies are very young they are hungry and milk is their only food, but later on after they eat other foods they like to suck. If there is milk, that is good, but if there is no milk they still like to suck.

We took good care of our children. A baby was almost always with its mother. We would carry the baby in a net bag wherever we went. We put leaves, usually banana leaves because they are soft, in the bottom of the net bag and lay the child on them. That was for carrying the baby. When it was not in the net bag, we held it. We would stroke the skin. Would put it up in the air. We would make baby noises at it. Baby boys went fully naked and baby girls just had a few bark strings hanging in front. So we could kiss the babies a great deal. Kiss all parts of their bodies—even little girls' cunts.

When my oldest children were small we carried them in the net bags. The leaves not only were soft but if the baby shit on them they could be thrown away. We didn't know about diapers. When the baby shit, we would just clean it up. Take our hand and wipe it off. If the shit fell on us, we would wipe that off with our hand or with leaves. We had no cloth for that. Children often shit on their mothers or someone else who held them. We thought nothing of it.

Only if a baby shit on its maternal uncle was it bad. And this was a very bad thing to have happen. If a baby soiled his mother's brother, this was very embarrassing for the baby's mother and father. They would have to give a big present to the man. This did happen sometimes. An uncle would like to hold his nephew or niece and maybe the baby would shit then. This would cause great shame to the child's father. He would have to give big pay to his brother-in-law if this happened. This was a big thing with all the Tairora.

Except for this one occasion we did not get angry with children if they pissed and shit around. Even when they were able to walk we let them do it where they wanted to. If it was in the house, we would clean it up for them. In those days, and still today in the villages, children shit and piss on the floor of the house until they are quite old. Even women do it sometimes at night if they have to. They are afraid to go out doors after dark and so they just go on the floor. Then they clean it up in the morning.

In Kainantu we don't do this any more. Little children wear diapers most of the time. Or if a mother sees her child wants to shit she will quickly put a cloth under it. Or she will let the shit fall on the ground and then shovel it up. Even in Kainantu this sometimes happens. We also have latrines that everyone is supposed to use. But the seats are too high for very little children. But in the villages people still use their houses at night if they have to go. And children are not punished for doing it in the house.

The other day Ika's son was lying on a bed in our house. He let one leg dangle over the edge of the bed and then he just shit on the floor. I was angry with him and yelled to Ika to come and clean it up right away. This is not the right thing to do anymore. So Ika and Mando came and cleaned it up but they didn't punish the boy, who is seven years old.

People assumed that children would see what older people did about shitting and that someday they would learn where to do it. They were not punished about it until they were quite old. A boy, however, after he was nine or ten must be careful of where he shit. He must be as careful as big people because from then on a sorcerer could use his shit, as well as other things, to make black magic on him, to make him sick, and to make him die. After this he was big and must take care that no one got his shit, just like all big people, so that no harm could befall him on this account.

Oten is coming to talk with you today. You want to talk with the old women. But you won't learn much. Old women don't think straight. They can talk about working in the garden, having babies, taking care of children, cooking food, taking care of pigs. But that is all they can talk about. They are still in the old ways. The ways we had before the White man came. Now that the government is here women know about more things than they used to. But the old ones haven't changed. If you want to learn about our ways, even those from before, the younger women are better. They can talk better to you.

For the Greater Glory

ONE TIME IN 1948, AFTER YEBI WAS BORN (SHE WAS STILL a baby but not tiny), two other women, highland women like me married to coastal men, and I went over to the compound to visit at Akro's house. He was by then the official Tairora interpreter for the government and he lived at the compound in Kainantu although he also kept a house in his village and often went out there. But this time he and his wife, Eto, were at the compound and we three women went over to visit them one evening. It was a moonlit night. Paulo and Yebi were asleep when I left the house and Robaga was home, so I thought it would be all right for me to go over there for a visit.

While we were there Akro cooked some rice and he was just dishing it up for us to eat when Robaga came in and started to scuffle with the three of us women. He began to hit us with his hands. I picked up a stick and hit him on the hand and hurt it. Then I ran away with the stick still in my hand. Later on he had to pay the other two women one pound each because he had hurt them. He was very angry.

After I got home I found out that the children had not wakened, they had not been crying, and Robaga really didn't need me at home. He was just cross because I had gone out to visit. He was mad just because I had gone out although I told him I was going with the other two women to Akro's house. He was mad about it though, and he came after me.

I was cross about the way he acted and I was also ashamed that he had acted this way but I didn't let him know how I felt. I was very nice to him, nicer than usual. I flattered him and made him feel good. The next night I said, "Let's sleep out in the cook house tonight. It was all my fault, I was to blame, I was wrong.

You were not wrong. You were right to come after us. It was all my fault."

While we were seated by the fire, talking, Robaga made some tea and we drank it. Then I asked him to tell me a story from the coastal area where he grew up, from the Sepik. Their stories are different from ours, and sometimes when we were first married he would tell me stories about the coast. This night I asked him to tell me one.

Before this, I had taken my best clothes out of the wooden box in which I kept them and put them under my pillow. After a while I said, "Let's make a big fire. It's the dry season now and it will be cold tonight. Let's make a big fire." And I put a lot of wood on the fire. Paulo and Yebi were there and also Nonu. Those three slept on one side of the fire. I told Robaga to sleep on the other side and I would sleep by the wall.

The fire was big, it got quite hot and we all got sleepy. Everyone but me went to sleep. They were all dead in sleep. I got up very quietly and went outside to pee. Then I came back inside. No one heard me. I took a rope, a three-pound rope, and measured it and tied it to a rafter so I would strangle when I fell on the floor. I coughed. No one stirred. I coughed again to make sure that they weren't awake. I wanted to be sure they were all really asleep and not just half asleep so they would wake up. I coughed again but no one stirred so I knew they were all asleep. I put on my best blouse and skirt. I tied the skirt on over my underpants and old skirt. I tied it tight so the blood wouldn't get all over everything. Then I washed my face and combed my hair.

I put the rope around my neck and then I jumped. My wind went sssssssst. I had hung the rope over a big plank that went across the room high up. When I fell the whole house shook a bit and ashes blew up from the hearth. The thatch roof shook. I became unconscious.

Soon Nonu awoke. He saw me. He rushed over to me, stooped down and reached under my legs and lifted me up. He cried out to Robaga, "Anyan has hung herself, I think she's dead!" He held me. He tried to cut the rope or get it loose but he couldn't because it was the kind with a wire inside of it. The noise of his axe chopping at it woke Robaga. He got up and loosened the rope. Nonu held me up by the legs with my head hanging down trying to get me to start breathing. Robaga ran out and called for help. He said that a woman had tried to hang herself. Then they took me to the infirmary. Gave me air. Mata Paro gave me air. Then I regained consciousness.

I felt weak for a while, I couldn't walk well and my neck was very sore. The rope had scraped my neck. You can still see this dark mark around my neck that was left by the bruise the rope made. In a few days I was all right again. Robaga was very unhappy about this. He did not get angry with me for quite a while after that.

Robaga is a Roman Catholic but there were none of their missionaries here. He was baptized when he was still in the Sepik area. Up here the Lutherans and the Seven Day Adventists baptize people. The Catholics made a station near Abiera in 1951. They decorated the place and all, but the mission was never built. Mando wouldn't give the land to the missionary. Because of this Robaga has been cross with Mando for a long time. Robaga often brings this up to Mando and scolds him for not having given land to the Catholics.

When I first went into Kainantu to live, our house was over near the Seven Day mission. I would see the missionaries and they were good to us but I didn't go to any classes. I didn't want to become a Seven Day. After we moved we were nearer Raipinka, where the Lutheran mission was located. The catechists would also come into Kainantu and have church and they wanted people to become Lutherans. After I had had Paulo and Yebi I became a Lutheran. In 1951 several of us went together. First, my name was put in a book. It was written down in a book. Then after that I would go to learn stories from the catechist.

The mission had a thatch house in Kainantu which was the church and we would go there to learn stories from the catechist. I learned about Noah and the ark; about Cain and Abel; about striking the rocks and water coming out, and other stories. The catechist also told us about God and Jesus. He also told us to be good so that we could go up above after we die and not down below where there is a big fire that will burn us up.

I was in the third group that was baptized. I was very frightened because I was afraid that my spirit would be angry with me for leaving the way of the Tairora and becoming a Lutheran. I went to learn the stories for a long while. Then in 1953 I was baptized. One Thursday all of us who were going to be baptized went to the church and there a catechist heard us talk about bad things we had done. He said, "You must get rid of your sins. Now you must tell me about all the bad things you have done in the past, about your sins. Then you will be baptized and you can be a good person." He took us into the church one by one. We did not all go together. We waited around outside for the catechist to call us in one at a time and talk to him.

When it was my turn I was very, very frightened. I was so scared I could not speak. My mouth was locked. The catechist said, "You must tell me about all your sins, if you have seduced a man, if you have stolen anything from someone else, something that didn't belong to you. If you have any sin, any bad thing that you have done, you must tell me about it. It is no good for you to hide this sort of thing. If you do, if you don't tell me what bad things you have done, you can't be baptized and you won't be a good person."

I was so scared I could hardly talk. I told him that I was an impatient woman, that I had never known my real mother. I told him that my mother's brother had brought me up and that I was often cross. I told him I didn't know how to steal, that I never did it. But I was so scared I couldn't talk well. All the time I was there I looked down at my hands or my legs. I wrung my hands together and I twisted my hair a lot and pulled at it very hard. If I didn't have strong hair it would have come out and I would be bald like Robaga.

The catechist kept telling me that I should not be ashamed. That I should get rid of my sins. I perspired a great deal. There was not just a little bit of sweat but a lot. It ran down me, down my face, down my sides, my front and back. Also I could not breathe well, I was short of breath and it was very hard to talk. My mouth was dry, my tongue wouldn't move very well. After a while, though, I was able to tell of one wrong doing.

When I was a little girl, Taria, Ika, Haru, and I took a pig of Mando's. Haru was still a baby. He could just barely walk. We took Mando's pig, tied its legs together and took it inside a house. We played with it, hit it, tickled it, and stuck reeds into its nose. This suffocated the pig and it died. After it died we took it out into the long grass. I carried it on my head. It was hard work for me to do, because it was so heavy. It was a good sized pig. I put it down and told Taria and Ika to look after it and then I went back to get Haru who could not walk very well yet.

Then the four of us went to the garden where Mando and Taramao were working and we told them that we had found the pig dead. They ran to see the pig and when they saw it they knew it had not died naturally. At first they accused us of beating it to death, of beating it in the head or the belly. We said no, that we hadn't beaten it at all and when they looked at the pig they knew we were telling the truth.

But Mando also saw the nose and knew what we had done to it. He was cross but he did not hit us. He talked to us a long time about how to treat pigs and that we shouldn't be mean to pigs and shouldn't tease them or put things in their nose because pigs were very good things to have. We should be good to pigs. Then Mando said we could have the pig to eat. Ika's father cooked the pig in an earth oven for us and then we ate it. We did not eat it all alone but other people came and a feast was held. It was a good pig.

I told the catechist this and then he wanted me to tell more things. But I couldn't talk. I couldn't think of anything else to tell him. I was very frightened. I was short of breath and I couldn't talk or think well. The catechist told me that there must be other things I could tell—hadn't I slept with a man not my husband and hadn't I stolen things that did not belong to me? He said, "God's child is here, Jesus is here, he is listening. He knows if you are not telling the truth. You must tell more sins." But I couldn't. So he said I could leave.

I went outside and lay down on the grass and cooled off. The catechist had told me not to talk with the others, those waiting outside who hadn't yet confessed. He didn't want us to let each other know what we talked about. He was afraid that if we did the ones that had not yet gone inside would just tell him the same stories that we had told him. So he didn't want us to talk with the people who had not yet gone in to confess. It would not do a person any good if he told someone else's story. He must tell about his own sins. That is what the catechist told us.

On Saturday all the natives took a lot of food to the church at Raipinka. Many people gathered there and they brought a lot of food. The next morning, Sunday, about 4 o'clock, we all went down to the Ramu River to wash ourselves. Then we went back up to the mission station and put on our best clothes and ornaments. I had bought new clothes at Tudor's store.

After we were all dressed up we went to the church and sat down. We sat on benches, the men on one side of the church and the women and children on the other side. We were very quiet and we didn't look around. The catechist had told us many times that we should walk with our heads bowed. We were not to look at other people. We were not to look at each other to see how nice we looked in our new clothes and jewelry. We were not to look at all the people that had come to watch us get baptized.

Then Johannes, the minister, came in and stood up in the front of the church. One row of people would stand up and all walk up and stand in front of Johannes. Johannes wet us with water that was kept in a glass bowl. After he had put water on all of us we went back and sat down. He told us that we should be quiet for five days and five nights. "Let the water soak into your skins before you go back to work." That is what he told us. Then we left. After five days we came back to the church and Johannes told us that now we must be good all the time, we must not steal anymore, we must not sleep with anyone but our husband, we must be good. "You are baptized. You must not sin again."

So I was baptized but that was all. I don't go to church and I don't follow what the mission said. I don't follow their beliefs.

Robaga is a Catholic and he did not want me to go to take communion after I was baptized. He and I have had a lot of arguments over this. Even though I have been baptized Robaga doesn't want me to take communion. He was baptized a Catholic when he still lived on the coast. He wants me to wait until a Catholic missionary settles here so we can be married properly. Robaga says he will give me a ring for my finger and then we will be married the correct way by a Catholic missionary. He doesn't want me to go to the Lutheran church even though I have been baptized a Lutheran.

One thing the catechist told us many times was that we should forget most of our old ways, our old beliefs. He said that our stories were wrong. They were bad and we should forget about them. We should just remember the stories we learned from the mission. We should even forget stories that didn't have a lesson. In the old days many stories told us how to behave. What were good ways and what were bad ways. But there were stories that were just stories. This is one of them, the story of a woman who married a dog.

A woman was taking care of her child, who was five or six years old. His father had died. The child made some arrows and shot some birds. He caught the birds but he gave only one to his mother. The mother said, "You are my child. You are not another person's child. I wanted to have you very badly. I suffered a lot when you were born. I am not like a stepmother to you. You hunted some animals and you ate them. Now, you go get a little something and bring it back to me."

The child left. The mother cooked some sweet potatoes on the fire. Then she left the house and went to the village of the dogs. She married a dog. Her child came back to the house and said, "Mama." There was no answer. He saw only the sweet potatoes. Then a little bug spoke to him. The boy said, "What?" The bug said, "I have gone away." The child answered, "Oh, oh, oh." He thought it was his mother speaking. The bug shouted out again. The child answered, "Oh, oh, oh." Then he stopped talking. He was very sorry for his mother. The bug spoke and the boy heard him. His mother was gone.

The child got some arrows. He put them in a small net bag. He took the arrows and followed his mother. He walked and walked and walked. Then he stopped and sent an arrow in one direction to find his mother. The arrow came back. It did not find his mother. Then he shot it in another direction. Again it came back. It did not find his mother. He kept on shooting the arrow in different directions. But it always came back to him. Finally, the arrow did not come back. It had found his mother.

The mother was working in her garden. She saw the arrow. She said, "Where did this arrow come from?" She put the arrow in her net bag and hung it on the fence. The child followed the arrow. He found his mother. His mother was digging in the garden. She worked with a digging stick. The child stood and watched her. After the work was finished the mother gathered all the digging sticks and hid them in the long grass. Then she went back to the village.

The child stayed at the garden. He broke all the digging sticks but one. He kept only one. It was a strong one. Then he hid. In the morning his mother came back. She looked and looked. "I hid the digging sticks. Where did they go?" she asked. She was thinking about work. She wanted the sticks. She couldn't find them. She pushed the long grass back with her hands and looked for the sticks. Then she saw the child. She said, "Where did you come from?"

That night she left the child in the long grass. She thought, "I am married to a dog not to a man. This is not really my child now." She went back to the garden. She said to the child, "Come along, we will go to the village together." At the house they cooked sweet potatoes and they ate. They left some of the sweet potatoes on the fire for her husband. The child and his mother sat by the fire.

When the dog husband came and took the sweet potatoes, the child hit him with a stick. The dog yelped and went outside. Then he went to the men's house (the house of the dogs). He talked to all of the other dogs that were there. After he had finished speaking he came back and said to the boy, "You get your bark blanket and your wooden head rest and we two will go to the men's house." The mother said, "All right, you get your things and go to the men's house."

But the mother's co-wife said to the boy, "No, you can't go. You stay here." The mother said, "Don't mind her. You go to sleep in the men's house." The co-wife said, "No, no, your child has come here and he should sleep with you." The mother said, "No, you go to the men's house." So the child went to the men's house.

The mother said, "I want to sleep now." The co-wife said, "You can't sleep now. Your child has gone to the men's house." The mother said, "I want to sleep now." And she slept. After a while the child screamed. The dogs were eating him. Ate him up. Only one finger joint remained. That and blood, strong, thick blood near the center post of the men's house. The mother slept. The dog husband slept.

In the morning he came to the mother. The mother said, "Where is the child?" The dog said, "Early this morning he took his bark blanket and left. It isn't good for him to stay with the other children." The dog talked that way. The co-wife said, "Yesterday I told you that the child should not sleep in the men's house." Now he is lost. The mother pretended to be asleep. She turned her face to the wall with her back to the other two and she cried. She cried for her child. The dog husband went away.

The next morning the co-wife said, "The two of us shouldn't go to work today. We'd better stay here." And the two stayed. All the dogs went to work in the forest. Only the two women remained in the village. They went into the men's house. They got the finger joint and the blood of the child. Then they got a banana stalk and planted it together with the finger joint and blood. They planted one banana. A good banana tree grew. Really good. It grew up in one day. The two women went to sleep. The next morning the banana already had fruit. The banana stalk was badly bent, it was close to breaking. The two women felt it and they looked at it and said, "The banana is broken. It is broken inside."

When they looked again, two brothers appeared. Two good little boys came out of the banana. They were really good. They came to the house of the women. "We want to help you," they said. The two boys talked to the two women. "You get bows and arrows ready. Get bracelets ready. Get everything ready for us."

The two women went to cut a bow. They worked very fast. They hurried like a machine. Worked very fast. Made arrows. Wove bracelets. They hurried everything. They made many things and put them by the house. When the two boys came back, the women said, "We have prepared everything for you." Then the boys said, "You get a lot of food and bring it. We can have it to eat. Then in the evening we can shut and lock the door against all the dogs. We two can fight." The women did as they were told. They got everything ready. Everything.

In the evening, the husband of the two women left. Then the two boys came back. They checked out the men's house. All the dogs were inside. The dogs called for a fire. Not just one asked for firewood, but all of them called out. The door was locked. Two dogs went up the center post of the house and wanted to come down. The boys shot them with arrows. Another dog tried to come out and the boys shot him. Two dogs came out and both of them were shot. All the dogs were killed. The two boys and their mothers came and looked to make sure that all of the dogs had been killed. Then the two women and the two boys went back to their own village.

If a woman's husband dies we think it is right for her to marry her husband's brother. But it is not good for her to have an affair with him while her husband is living. It is not good. In 1946, Bohaname, a Tongera woman had an affair with her husband's younger brother. They played together and fucked. This went on for quite a while. When the husband discovered it he was very angry. He got some of his close male relatives and they were very hard on Bohaname. They beat her with canes. They heated wires on the fire and put them on her back to burn her meat and then they would lift the burned flesh off. They smeared dog and pig shit all over her. They hit her. They also told her that she must work, work, work, that she must work harder than ever.

This treatment went on for a while. She asked them to stop mistreating her. She pleaded with them. She said she didn't mind having to work so hard but the physical torture was more than she could take. They didn't stop, though. They all kept on hitting her and burning her and all the other things. Also, a lot of people talked about her. They said she had done wrong and that it was good that she should pay for it. This shamed her very much. Finally, she could stand this no longer and she hung herself.

Bohaname was her husband's only wife at that time. If a man has two or more wives, he should be good to all of them. He should treat them the same way. He should play and fuck with all of them. If he doesn't and if one of them has an affair with another man, people won't be so hard on her. They will say that a woman isn't like a stick of wood. She needs to play and fuck, and they will not be so hard on her if her husband doesn't give her this and she goes with another man and has fun with him. She still should not do it with her husband's brother though.

Some men treat all their wives well and some don't. Hantako, a woman from Arogara, was married to a Kamano man who was a doctor's aide. They lived at Kainantu. The husband also had another wife, a Kamano woman whom he had married first. Because of his work he didn't spend much time in Kainantu. He was usually stationed at a first-aid station out in various villages. He would take his first wife with him and leave Hantako in Kainantu all alone.

One afternoon Hantako came over to my house and we cooked food in an earth oven. At this time Hantako told me that a rat had been nibbling on some of the things in her house—her net bag, sweet potatoes, and other things—and she wanted to bring them over to my house and leave them there so the rats would not get them. She said that she was then going to Arogara to visit her relatives.

I said that she shouldn't bother to get them then, but she should bring them over the next day. She agreed but soon she changed her mind and did it that very afternoon. After she brought the things over to my house we went down to the river for water and after we brought it back Hantako went to her house.

That night Hantako made a big fire in her house. Abo was there too. The fire was very hot and Abo slept well. Hantako took off her clothes, the cotton clothes that she wore while living in Kainantu, and put on her old clothes—her village skirt, woven armlets, and net bag. She fastened a rope around a roof pole and around her neck, put her foot on Abo's neck so she wouldn't get up, and then she hung herself. When Abo did awaken about ten o'clock she shouted to Hantako's husband, who was sleeping in a nearby house. He called Doctor Zigas, who tried to get her to breathe but they couldn't. She was dead. They were going to bury her in Kainantu but her relatives came to get her and took her to Arogara for burial. Hantako was older than I am and she had no children. Her co-wife had three children.

As I told you, Baho was also engaged to Titio, my first husband, but she had not yet been married at the time that he died. It was common among us for a woman, after her husband died, to marry her husband's brother. This was very true when there were children that had already been born. It was not good to take children away from their father's relatives, and so a woman would marry one of the brothers of her husband and continue to live at the village of the husband's relatives. This is where the children belonged. If the mother tried to take the children away, if she wanted to marry someone else, the husband's relatives would be very angry, really hot in the belly. They would say, "That child is our blood, our semen. It doesn't belong to you." The mother was supposed to stay and marry in that village. After the children were grown up she could marry to some other village if she still wanted to.

Although Baho was not yet married when Titio died, just engaged, she did marry one of Titio's brothers. However, he didn't take good care of her so she left him. She is now married to Bebo, but before that, after she left Titio's brother, she went to Aiyura to stay with Otan. While she was there one of the White men asked her if she wanted to come sleep with him. She said yes. She continued to live with Otan but she would go up to the master's house at night and sleep with him.

The master didn't give her anything for this—no money, no clothes, nothing. This is the fashion of the White man as well as the Black man. They want to get sexual favors for nothing if they can. After a while Baho got sick and had to go into Kainantu to the infirmary. When she got well she lived with Robaga and me at our house for quite a while. All during that time she slept with the doctor. The doctor gave her a laplap and a knife. After a while Baho thought, "I don't like this way, I don't have a name, I don't like this way." And she came back to the village and married Bebo.

Not many young husbands have more than one or two wives now. Lai has three and Manko has three, but most of the men who have three or more wives are older men. The wives get along with each other pretty well but sometimes they fight.

A while ago there was a big fight near here. Minie and two of her daughters were working in their garden. Otube and Bobara were working in a garden nearby. Some of the children laughed at Bobara because some of his toes are cut off. There was a big fight. Lots of talk and shouting and name-calling. Then Otube and Minie started to really fight and Otube pulled off all of Minie's skirts. Minie was very embarrassed and sat right down on the ground and put her hands over her genitals. She stayed there until her daughter brought her a skirt to put on. Then her other daughter got into the fight with Otube and hit her so hard she broke her arm.

This case was taken to court. The *luluai* and the *tultul* didn't tell the right story, so Minie was put in jail instead of her daughter. Otube is still in the infirmary but after she gets out she will go to jail to finish her four months of time

To the Coast: *Another First*

AFTER I MARRIED ROBAGA I USED TO WONDER WHAT HIS native village was like. I asked him many questions. What kind of houses did the people live in? What food did they eat and how did they cook it? What did people do? I asked him about all sorts of things. "Do you live in houses with metal roofs?" "No," he would say, "our houses are like yours."

Robaga had visited my village several times so he knew what it was like and what we did there. But I had not seen his village and I wondered about it. Finally, in 1952, I took my first trip to the coast. We were planning to go to Robaga's village on the coast but because there was a big sickness there at the time, we could go only to Madang. It was my first trip to the coast.

Robaga, Paulo, Yebi, and I all went together. I was pregnant at the time. Robaga got his pay, $22.00, plus $4.50 for his rations. In addition the doctor gave him $4.50 to buy some things for him. We flew on a big Qantas airplane and the government paid our way. On the trip Paulo and Yebi vomited several times. We had our dog with us and he vomited too. Robaga and I didn't vomit. When we came near Madang I saw what I thought was smoke from a huge grass fire. I thought that the people must burn great big patches of grass at one time and the smoke covered everything as far as I could see. But Robaga said, "No, That's the ocean." It was the first time I had seen the saltwater and it looked like smoke. I thought they were burning grass.

While we were on the coast I felt awful. It was too hot there. My whole body ached. I didn't do anything. I thought about my village, about all my friends. I would talk to Robaga about my village, how I missed it. I wanted to go home. Robaga said, "No, you can't go back now. The government didn't send us for nothing. It's no good that you return to your village and I stay on here alone. I have some things to do. I have my name to live up to. It wouldn't be right for me not to have you and the children with me."

Robaga spoke that way, so I stayed. But I didn't like the food, and I didn't eat much. I just cried. That's all I did. I felt hot. Robaga said, "You are talking nonsense. You straighten up." I said, "I don't want to do anything. I don't like to walk around." Robaga said, "It's no good for me to walk around on the roads while you take it easy." I said, "Next time I'll stay at my village. I don't like it here. Another time you can come here alone." That's what I said.

While we were on the coast I did see a few things. I saw some ships, great big ships. We didn't go on any of the big ships but we did have a ride in a canoe and I was terribly frightened. I was afraid it would tip over and then what would I do? I went to some stores run by Chinese and they had a lot of goods in them. They were much, much bigger than the stores we have in Kainantu. I used to go inside and look at the things. I didn't go into any of the stores that belonged to the White man though.

We bought a few things: two pair of shorts for Paulo, some kerosene, some crackers and some bread, but not much else. We just looked most of the time. The open air markets there were much bigger than any I had seen. People brought food of different kinds to one place to sell it. These markets were very large and covered a lot of ground.

They had movies in Madang at that time but we were afraid to go. I rode in a Jeep for the first time. I was frightened by that too. I did not ride very far, not enough to get sick the way some people do the first time they ride in a car.

Some of the houses were a bit like ours but many were up on stilts. They were not built on the ground like ours but raised up on poles. I had not seen many houses with metal roofs before then, but there were a lot in Madang. I did not like the coast, mainly because it was too hot. I caught malaria while I was there, although I did not have it very badly.

Robaga told me that his village on the Sepik River would be a little like the coast. We wanted to go to the Sepik but we couldn't that first time because of the big sickness the people were having there then. We stayed in Madang for two weeks and then came back to Kainantu in a small biplane. Robaga gave the money back to the doctor because we hadn't bought anything for him. I was glad to get back home because I didn't like the coast. Not that first time. It was not any good at all. That's what I thought.

Several years later I visited the coast again. We went to the Sepik area as well as to Robaga's village, Batika, which is up the mountains a bit back from the sea. That time I took a net bag filled with sweet potatoes because I remembered how I had missed them in Madang. When I had eaten the sweet potatoes I wanted more. I didn't like the food they had on the coast. I bought some sweet potatoes at a market but they were very dear and they were small and not very good.

Of the foods that I ate for the first time on the coast I liked coconuts, fish, and a small eel. But I thought sago was disgusting, and that's what they eat so much of. One time in a market I was going to buy some shark meat but Robaga told me not to because he said I wouldn't like it. On this trip I met Robaga's brothers and sisters. I had never met them. His parents were dead. His father died when Robaga was young and his mother died after he went to the highlands to live. I had met his mother's relatives the first time in Madang. I met lots of his relatives on these trips to the coast.

On the way back from the Sepik we went to Wewak on a ship, and that was awful. I didn't like it at all. It's the only time I've been on a ship. I felt terrible. I couldn't eat. One time when I had to go to the toilet Robaga offered to help me so I wouldn't fall. I felt so awful that I told him not to bother about me. When he said that he didn't want me to fall in the ocean I said that it didn't matter if I died, if my name stopped forever.

Robaga had to take care of Paulo and Yebi most of the time because I was so sick. Paulo didn't vomit but Yebi did. I was sure I was going to die, but I didn't care. After we finally got off the boat, for a day or two it felt as if the ground were moving under me. My legs just wouldn't work right. It all didn't feel right and I could not walk well for a couple of days.

I have been to the Sepik three times, to Goroka, Madang, Wewalk, Sepik, and back. Twice I have gone to Lae and we saw Gusap, Dumpu, and Kaiapit on the way. Here in the highlands I have been to Moke as well as Goroka. And when I was a little girl I went to Barabuna once and could see as far away as Suwaira. I also went to Batainabura once and to Onamucca once.

I was the first person from my village to go to the coast. I was one of the first Tairora to go. That was in 1952. In 1954 some young men went to the coast to work, including Haru and Amuri. A woman from Bontaa, who is married to an Arogara, has gone. Otan has been to Wewak with her husband, who came from there. An Arogara woman who is married to a Manus man has been there. Five women from Haparira and Ontabura went to Popondetta with their husbands when they went there to work in 1958, I think.

My fourth child was born in 1952 and Robaga named him Simi. I had no trouble when he was born. He came very quickly and that was all. Only with the first child did I have any trouble, and even with him it was not too bad. But Simi was born quickly. He was born in Kainantu. I did not go back to Abiera for his birth. Only Paulo was born there.

The feast that we had for Simi's birth was given in Kainantu. People came into Kainantu from Abiera for the feast. Simi was a strong child. You remember seeing him in 1954. He was a strong baby but he died very suddenly in 1956 when he was only four years old. He was not sick at all but a sorcerer gave him some poisoned cookies. I think he caused the death of my third baby, the one that died right after it was born, and also Simi's death. I am sure he caused it. But he hasn't done anything to me or any of my family since 1956.

When my third baby, a girl, died we didn't give any gifts to my relatives. But when Simi died, Robaga paid them well. He gave $34.00, two pigs, and four pieces of cloth to my relatives and they divided them up. Robaga paid them very well.

Simi was the youngest of my children then and we were very sorry when he died. He was a strong child and was poisoned. He was not sick at all before that. He just died suddenly. We tried to take the case to court. But the *kiap* said, "No." He was like most *kiaps*. He didn't believe in sorcery. So he said this case couldn't come to court.

After he died I had four more children. Hinda was born in 1955 and it was Bano, my father, who gave her her name. Anto, another girl, was born in 1957 and Robaga gave her her name. In 1959 I had another baby boy and we named him Simi, the name of the boy who had died. This is a custom of ours. If a baby or child dies the parents are very sorry about it. Also they like the name the child has. So if they have another child of that sex, they give this child the name of the one who is dead. This happens very often with us.

Wanama, my baby, was born in 1962 and Paulo gave her the name. He named her after my mother. The feasts of all my children except Paulo, the first, were held at Kainantu. All of the children except Paulo were born there too.

It was Ika who threw away the cord from Simi. Aroba did it for Hinda and Anto. They tied the dried cord to an arrow. Then they shot the arrow toward the mountain up past Kaagawta. I still have the cord of Wanama. It is in this little pink knit sack and I carry it with me in my tin. I have it with me all the time and don't know yet who will send it away. I think either Aroba or Ika will do it.

Another thing about the children that I have not told you is about the net bags they were carried in. It is common to have a new net bag for a baby, but I didn't have a new one for Paulo. Just used an old net bag that I had. But before Yebi was born I made a new net bag just for her and carried her in it when she was a baby. I had a new net bag for each of the rest of my children. The ones for Hinda, Anto, and the two Simi's, I bought at the trade store run by the mission. I made the net bag for Wanama.

You see this piece of tree bark? It is the kind that village women chew if they don't want to have children. Eki gave it to me the other day. She told me that I have had enough children. That eight children is a lot. She said that I should take it easy from having children. She said that if I chew this I won't have more. But I haven't chewed it and I don't intend to. This is something for village people. I don't believe in this any more. I now drink tea, eat rice, eat tinned meat, and wear cotton clothes. I don't do many of the things that the villagers do and I won't chew this bark. But village women that don't want to have more children will chew this and other plants. They believe it will work for them.

All men and women have dreams but some dream more than others. Some people dream a lot and some people don't. They dream about food, their gardens, their relatives, their ancestors, animals, dances—all of these things they can dream about. Some people remember their dreams a long time and some forget them quickly. Some people make songs about their dreams and they will sing them. If other people like a song they sing it too, and some of them are sung by everybody at our dances.

Some people do things to make good dreams. It is good to have a human bone to put under your pillow and that will make good dreams.[7] After I knew that Bano was my father he gave me a rib of Matoto. It was not like our regular rib bones but it was a great big one, like a cow or horse. I could put it around my side and it would reach from the middle of my back to the middle of my chest. I slept on this bone for a year. I would put it under my pillow or by my side each night. I had some dreams but they were not about Matoto. I didn't see him. His rib bone didn't work for me. So I returned the bone to Bano.

A few years ago in Kainantu I had a dream and I made a song out of it. I dreamt that I was a young girl at home with my mother. There was a lot of food and we ate it. At that time I went around a lot with the other girls. One day I noticed that my companion was missing. I went to find her. I came to a big rock. It was like a big piece of metal. There was a lot of water running around it and there was a big hole inside it. The hole was filled with men that had turned to dogs. Two dogs guarded the entry at the top of the hole. I was very frightened. I asked them if they had seen my friend. They said I could go inside and look if I wanted to. I said, "No. I don't want to go inside. You go look for me and see if she is there." They told me that they thought she had gone inside but they weren't sure. They said I should go in and look. I thought about it. I was afraid. But finally I decided I would go in. I had to walk through deep water. I was carrying some firewood. I put it on my head and tried to use my hands to keep my balance as I walked through the deep water. I couldn't move though. That is, I would move my legs but I didn't get anywhere. Just stayed in the same place. The dogs didn't help me at all. I worked and worked and worked but I couldn't get anywhere. Finally I stopped trying and then I woke up. I remember that I thought the dogs had eaten my friend and I told them so and they laughed. Later on I told this dream to people and I made a song of it. People laughed at it and said I shouldn't try so hard to find my friend.

A few nights ago I had this dream and you were in it. I went to a strange place and dug two big holes. I saw the bones of a man in the first hole. I saw bones of a man in both holes. I left them and went back to the village. While I was gone all the men had cut the tail and the balls of my pig. When I saw that I was angry. I said, "A long time ago Papa cut the ear of this pig. Who is it that now has cut the tail and the balls of my pig? I don't like this at all."

There was no answer. In a few minutes a big airplane appeared. It was close to the fence and I was frightened. I said to the airplane, "Don't come close to the fence or you will break it." Then you said to me, "Put on some powder, take my child, and we two will look at the airplane." I poured a lot of powder on my legs, hands, face, and hair. I put the powder all over my body. I put plenty of powder on, then I got your child and held her. You put on powder too, but you just put a little bit on your hands and face. I put plenty on, all over me, and then I held the baby.

At that point, Paulo, who was sleeping with me, peed in bed and the warmth of the pee on my ribs wakened me. I got up and was a bit cross with him for breaking my dream. I didn't hit him but I was cross with him. I said, "You are not a little boy. You are a big boy. You're big enough to get up and go outside to pee. You're not the same as a little boy who still sucks his mother's teat and who can't think for himself. You are big enough to get up and go outside."

I remember one dream that I had during the No good time, as we speak of the big war. An airplane flew up in the air right by me and frightened me very much. It didn't fly through the air as airplanes usually do. It came right up beside me. I was very frightened so I ran to the woods. There I saw a policeman. I turned and ran away from him and there was another policeman. Again I ran and saw another policeman. I ran another way and saw another policeman. Then I ran out onto the road. Two White men were standing in front of me so I turned and ran the other way. A car came along and I ran away from it. The driver of the car called out to me to come to the car but I was afraid. He called many times but I was afraid. But after a while I did go near the car. The driver asked me to get in the car. I said, "No." He tried to get me to go into the car but I didn't want to. Then my mother's brothers came along and I told them what had happened. They told me not to be afraid. They said that airplanes would all be like this now. That there would be airplane roads and airplanes would go on roads. They also told me that it was all right to get into the car and go for a ride. Then I woke up.

When Teba's ear was bitten off yesterday I was reminded of people eating human meat. As you know, Teba and Ire, whose husband Teba will marry when she is finished mourning for her first husband who died, had a big fight. Ire does not want her husband to take another wife, but he is the brother of Teba's first husband and he should marry her. The two women fought and Ire bit Teba's ear with her teeth and part of it fell off. When you and I got up there to see what was happening, Teba was looking around in the dirt for her ear. She wanted it, not to eat it, but to prevent a sorcerer from getting it and working black magic against her.

But there have been cases of people eating human meat. When Abe was very young he was adopted by Opu and his wife. It was they who brought him up. Abe knew his real parents, who lived in a different village, and he always wanted to go back to see his mother and father. He really wanted to go back and live with them. Opu was a stubborn man, he didn't want Abe to leave, he wanted him to stay with him. But Abe kept trying to run back to his parents.

Finally, Opu cut off his own earlobe and cooked it with greens.

He then chewed gingerroot, tree bark, and some other things, and spit this into the mixture of the ear meat and greens. Then he gave it to Abe to eat. After Abe ate it he wanted to stay with Opu and not run to his real parents. Opu knew that if Abe ate some of his flesh he would stay with him.

Another man who has eaten human flesh is the one you know about at Batainabura. You remember when Akaw told you of a time when he was a young boy. His father took him to Suwaira and while they were there there was a big fight between Suwaira and Obura. One of the most powerful men from Obura, one of their main warriors, was killed in that battle. Parts of his body were cooked and eaten. Akaw's father gave him some of the meat. He ate it and thought it tasted good. He did not know it was meat from a man. Later his father told Akaw what it was. He wanted Akaw to become a big strong man and a good fighter. And Akaw did become one of the best warriors at Batainabura. I had not heard about this until Akaw told it to you.

The "wind" first came up a long time ago, long long before World War II.[8] The "wind" was the belief by some of my people that if they did certain things they would no longer have to work. Food and everything would be given to them by the spirits of our ancestors. Just as the White man gets food without planting gardens so we would get it too. That was how some people thought. The first time I remember was like this. First of all most of the men and women at the village shook and shivered a great deal. They did not work in their gardens. They just went to the gardens to get food, then brought it back to the village and cooked it. A lot of pigs were killed. Many dogs were killed at that time too. All of the food was eaten. There were no special houses where all this was done; people just gathered at each other's houses. They chewed gingerroot and a condiment and then spit it into the food. They thought that then the ghosts of all dead men and women would bring them good things, that both men and women would travel to the place of the ghosts. They would go to Nomatera. They would get a lot of food ready, fill up their net bags, and then go. They ate the food themselves. They did not stay there long but would come back quickly. I remember that the people who shook, also fought and argued a lot. They fought and argued with each other. I don't remember everything too clearly, since I was very young, but I remember that much.

The second time this happened was in 1947. After the fighting had stopped and everyone knew that the fighting was finished, this belief came again. This time the men made wooden rifles and they marched around a great deal. They built special houses where they met to do this. They all thought that the ghosts of the dead would bring all the things that the White man has and we don't have and they would give them to all of us New Guineans. The men made wooden rifles. They practiced with them. They believed that later they would be given real ones and they were practicing with the wooden ones so they could use the rifles when they came. Both times it was not only our people that did it, but everyone in this whole area.

In 1953, before you came to Tairora, Damu, a Kamano woman, was walking along the road near Tampera. All of a sudden something hit her, it hit her hard. The skin on her left side was burned, the clothes on that side of her body were torn to shreds, her pandanus mat disappeared completely, her net bag and the sweet potatoes she had in it were shattered to bits. Damu thought that something came out of the ground and hit her, that someone put some sort of poison into the ground and it came out and hit her.

One woman saw Damu fall. She asked another woman to go with her to help Damu. The other woman wouldn't believe what the first one said, but thought she was fooling her. Finally the two went and they found Damu lying on the ground. Her voice was very weak. She could not move. The two women got an old man to carry Damu home. She was quite sick. She thought that something came out of the ground and hit her. It was during a storm that she was hit. She was struck by lightning.

The adultery that Arat told you I was involved in was not mine. Arat told you that a man from Tongera had seduced me and that we had had sexual intercourse together and that we will be sent to

jail. But she was just gossiping. What she said was not true. I will
tell you what really happened. Last week at Abiera my sister-in-law
and I went to get firewood. On the way we met her boyfriend, a
man who wanted to have an affair with her. I acted as go-between
and carried the messages back and forth between them. I didn't try
to stop them from fucking because that is their business, not mine.
They did have intercourse after that and have had it several times
since, I think. I did not tell on them. I don't know how her husband found out. They were called into court, but I was not. The
head man asked me about it but didn't take me to court. Just the
other two, the ones who had the affair. They are both in jail now
but I was not even called into court.

I did have an affair with Bora of Borawta though. That was before I worked for you. It was in 1953, and it was all finished when I
first worked for you. Bora worked at Kainantu then, he worked for
the *kiap*. He and his wife lived in Kainantu. He had only one wife
then, although now he has two and they live at Borawta. One of
Bora's jobs at that time was to go to Kamano territory over by
Javonka, and get wood. He and his wife were good friends of ours,
Robaga and me, and we often ate our meals together. Sometimes,
Bora would come over by himself to have lunch with Robaga and
me. I liked him a lot. Several times I cooked sweet potato for Bora
and would take it to him as he worked with the wood near
Javonka. Bora liked me too and he told me many times how much
he liked me. He would sit near me when he could. He would try to
touch my skirt. When I was near him I would put my fingers inside
his belt. I would not look directly at him but would look down at
the ground.

This is the way a man and a woman behave when they like each
other and want to have an affair. I was very bashful about it. That
is the way the woman is. She acts that way when she is in love with
a man who is not her husband. He flattered me, told me lots of
things to make me feel good, and he said he wanted to be my
lover. For a long while I said no, that I was married, had a good
man, and wouldn't sleep with him although I did like him. He
kept on asking me to do it. I would take him food, more and more

all the time. Finally, we did fuck. We did it many times. It went on for quite a while. I don't know if Robaga suspected what was happening or not. He didn't say anything about it.

Then, one evening several of us were walking along the road. Tao was behind me and Bora was behind Tao. Bora went around Tao, passed in front of him and alongside me. He touched my breast. I was surprised and I said, "Who is touching me?" Bora didn't say anything and he didn't do anything but Tao had seen and heard and he told Robaga about it. Robaga was very angry and he took the case to court. Both Bora and I were put in jail for a month. By then I really liked Bora a great deal. I wanted him more than I wanted Robaga. I wanted him very much.

While I was in jail, Robaga would bring food to me but I would not touch it. I would take food from Bora though, food that his wife brought to him. Bora's wife would get angry with him for giving food to me but he didn't care, he liked me and wanted me and continued to give me food. His wife had been cross with him about our affair but she hadn't been as bad as Robaga. She didn't behave about it as he did. While I was in jail I was very ashamed of being there. I was also disgusted with Robaga for the way he behaved. It was because of him that I was in jail and I was angry with him for behaving that way. So I wouldn't accept the food that he brought to me.

I was also cross with him because I had to leave the children. I had three of them then, and it was all because of him that I had to leave them. Robaga got so cross with me that he threatened to have me jailed again if I kept eating Bora's food and not taking his. One time Robaga even asked Tooke to tell me that I should forget about Bora and stay with him.

When our time in jail was up, we were taken over to the *kiap*'s office before we were freed. After the *kiap* told us we could go, we went back to the jail house to change our clothes. I did not wear a jail skirt, but I didn't have a blouse on when I went to the *kiap*'s and I went back to put one on and to get my comb, tin, and other things I had left there. Bora went back to change his laplap because he had worn a jail one.

We left the jail together and were walking along the road to Raipinka. Robaga was waiting for us all this time. Finally he came up to us and told me to come with him. I said, "No. I'm not going with you. I'm going with Bora." I didn't really mean it, but I was testing Robaga to see what he would do. He threatened to have us jailed again. He really didn't care if I was jailed again. He wanted Bora jailed but I wanted to be with Bora if he was going to be jailed.

Bora and I started out again toward Raipinka and Robaga walked along with us. He asked me to come spend the night with him and the children. I finally decided I would, because I wanted to be with the children. We all slept together that night at Paulo's house. That was Paulo, Robaga's friend from the Sepik. Paulo, my son, is named after him.

Robaga kept telling me to come back. He talked about the children and about a lot of things. He told me he wouldn't let me go. He said that when he married me I was just a village native. I wore a bark skirt, I braided and greased my hair, I was naked from the waist up. It was he, he said, who made a real woman out of me. He said that it was he who civilized me. He said he wasn't going to let me go now after all he had done to make me into a civilized woman. So, I decided to stay.

But I was still very fond of Bora and I was not happy with Robaga. I was also very much ashamed of what had happened. One time when I was visiting Abiera, I was staying with my father, Bano. One day some of us were sitting around the fire talking and chewing betel nut. I told them that I had to go to the toilet and I went out. But I didn't go to the latrine. I went up the hill. Gaharu saw me and wondered where I was going all alone. "What is she doing all alone?" he thought. "Is she going for firewood? Is she following another woman, perhaps?" So he asked at Bano's house and they told him that I had gone to the outhouse. Gaharu said that I wasn't out there and he told them where he'd seen me.

Ika ran after me and caught up to me before I went into the woods where I was going to hang myself. I wanted to kill myself because I was so embarrassed and unhappy over what had happened. But Ika caught up with me and took the rope that I was carrying away from me and took me back to the village. I did not try to kill myself again.

But men still think that women might kill themselves, especially those women who have tried it more than once. You remember the other day. You had gone down across the river and then climbed up to the big path on the mountainside. When you came back you met me. I was walking with Bampane's daughter who was carrying Wanama. When you got back to the village you told Ihube where I was. When Ihube looked and saw how far I had walked he thought I might be going to the woods to kill myself. He ran very fast to catch me. But I was not thinking of this at all. I was just out walking.

One time, after Robaga and I had had a fight, I came out to Abiera for a while. When Robaga came out to get me Himato told him that I had had another affair with Bora. But I hadn't. Bora had told Himato that he still liked me and that if Robaga ever left me or died that he, Bora, would like to marry me. We did not sleep together then. Robaga took the case to court but the *kiap* told him that the affair was finished.

Today I met Tibabara on the road as I was coming up here. She is the crazy woman who lives at Okamaka. You have seen her before. She was once married to an old man who has since died. She has not married again. She has had no children. She is really crazy. She has fits, she falls on the ground, jerks her arms and legs, and white water comes out of her mouth. Once when Tibabara had a fit she fell in the fire and burned herself badly. She still has no hair growing on the part of her head that was burned. She never keeps her skirts on properly; they are always hanging too far down in front or in back. You can see more of her butts than you should be able to, but she doesn't know any better. Some of the men from Aiyura screw her and don't give her anything for it. The Tairora men, though, are afraid to screw her. There are not many really crazy people here but Tibabara is one of them, really crazy. You remember I told you about a crazy woman at Abiera when I was growing up. How we would play with her. She also would shit and piss right on the fire in the houses. Pao of Arogara was crazy. They took him to Moresby, but he is back now.

Just last night I had this dream. There were two round lakes. One was a lot bigger than the other. The road to them was bumpy. But I wanted to go to the big one. When I got there I yelled. As I yelled my words went down below and then they came up again (echo). I kept looking at the water. I didn't want the water to splash in big waves around me. I said this as I went into the water. I was really afraid of this lake. The water was breaking very high. I wanted to be in the water even though my arms and legs ached because it was so cold, as cold as ice.

In the distance I saw a lot of men and women. They were on a great big ship. I called to the ship and it came near me. I talked to it. I wanted to look more, but my arms and legs were numb from the cold water. I took a piece of firewood and held it close to my arms and legs to warm them. The ship sailed around and around in the water. It was imprisoned in the water. I watched it.

There was a man standing near me. He was a big man. He had a boar tusk in his nose. He wore a breech clout; all the people wore the old kind of dress. I asked him, "Will the men catch me and put me on this ship?" He said, "No. They just want to get food. They don't want you. They just want food." I asked, "What food do they want?" He said, "All the men and women want to get their own food." I said, "Where? There is no land of theirs here." I kept on looking. I said, "I want to see the gardens. I want to see the food."

The man said, "The ship moves. It doesn't need a road. It just goes where the machine tells it to go. When it goes near the food they throw the food into the pipe and that pumps it into the ship." That is what the man who was standing near me told me. He also said, "We can't go near these people. They just want to get food. That is all." I said, "I want to watch them dump the food into the pipe. See them dump the food into the ship." I watched them do it.

As I looked I saw my name on some of the food they were going to take. I said, "My name is on some of that food. It is my name on the food. It is my food." I went near the ship and grabbed the food.

The people looked at me. They stared at me. They wanted to punish me. They wanted to cut my throat. I said, "I haven't taken anything of yours. I saw my name on it so I took the food that really belongs to me." But they still wanted to cut my throat. I said, "All right. You can cut my throat. I am not afraid. I haven't stolen anything that belongs to you. I saw food that belongs to me and I took it."

They still wanted to hurt me but the big man told them, "She doesn't know how to read, she doesn't know how to write. She thought she saw her name on the food and she took it. She can give it back to you." That is what he said to the people on the ship. I said to him, "Now I know for sure you do not want to help me. Now I know for certain that you are not telling the truth." Then my child pulled the blanket off me and I got cold. When I got up this morning I didn't feel very good.

One time when I was at Bontaa for a feast I met a Master along the road. He told me to bring sweet potatoes to his house and he would buy them. He said I could see his farm too. He told some of the other women the same thing. I told Robaga about it and he said it was all right to sell sweet potatoes to the Master. So I filled a net bag with sweet potatoes from my garden and took it down to his place. He was there and he bought the sweet potatoes for a shilling.

This was very poor pay since it was a big net bag filled with good sweet potatoes and I had carried it a long, long way. He didn't weigh it. He just gave me a shilling. Then he told me to come in the house and see it, to look around. I just stood in the doorway and looked. The foreman was standing in the room and the Master was sitting down. Again, he asked me to come inside. I said, "No. I'll stay here. I can see everything from here."

Again he asked me to come inside. But I said no. Then he told me that I couldn't see the bedroom from there and that I should go in the bedroom and look around. I said, "No. I don't want to go in there. I don't want to see it." Then he told me again to go into the bedroom. He said we could have fun together in there. But I told him, "No. I am already married. I have a man. I am married to a Sepik and I fuck with him."

The Master said that my man was a nobody and that I should forget about him and come sleep with him. I kept on saying "No." I was very insistent about it and I didn't sleep with him. When I got back to Kainantu I told Robaga about what happened and Robaga then went to the Master and asked him what he wanted with his wife. Robaga told him that I belonged to him (Robaga) and the Master should leave me alone. The Master laughed and said that he didn't know I was Robaga's wife. He said he didn't even know I was married, although I had told him that I was.

A lot of Masters who don't have their wives here do sleep with New Guinean women. The men who have their wives here don't sleep with local women. I suppose that is because they think their wives might get sick if they slept with a local woman and then slept with their wife. I don't know of any Master who has his wife here who has slept with a local woman, although there might be some. I don't know about all of them. A lot of Masters don't bring their wives with them though. We think that they have wives back in Australia but they don't bring them to New Guinea.

Some of the Masters here have taken local women to be their wives. The women live with the Master and the children belong to him. Some men have done this for a long time. The local women that are married to Masters live in good houses. They wear good clothes. Some of them even have shoes. Some of these Masters send their children to school too.

But we all know that if the Master ever goes back to Australia he will not take his New Guinean wife or the children with him. He will leave them here and she will go back to her village and live with her relatives or marry a local man. All the local women that are married to Masters know this. But there are some that have been married to Masters for a long time and the Masters say they won't go back to Australia but they will stay in New Guinea until they die. They say that New Guinea is their country now.

But a lot of Masters that don't have wives here just sleep with a local girl for a period of time—or they may have local girls in different places that they sleep with. There are many ways to do it. *Kiaps* sometimes get girls from the village. They'll give a boy something, a gift or money, and he'll bring his sister or some girl in. The girl will not wear her native skirt but will put on cotton clothes and take a bath and comb her hair and then come in. At night the boy will take her to the Master's house and she will go in and they will screw. Usually, the Master will send her away before it gets light.

There have been some women—one Chimbu that I know of—who sleep with both Masters and local men. She is a real whore. She used to go to the parties that the Masters would have. She would not really be a guest at the party but she would hang around outside or in the kitchen along with the local men who do this. This way she would get some food and be able to see the Master's party. After the party she would go home with one of the Masters and fuck with him. She slept with several Masters and local men; she wouldn't stay with just one for a long time.

Another way that it's done, a White man sleeping with a village girl, is for the man to give a large amount of pay to the family of the girl. He will do this for some girl that lives in a village close to his house. Then whenever he wants the girl to come over to his house he will send someone to tell her. She will get cleaned up, put on the clothes that he gave her, and go over to his house. But she doesn't live with him all the time. She is not married to him. But because he has given pay to her father or brothers, she must go and sleep with him when he wants her to.

Some Masters are very good about this but some aren't. One of the old Masters, one who has been here a long time, was not good about this. He would sleep with local women all the time but he would not marry them and he wouldn't have anything to do with the children that were born.

We all know about one of his daughters. She was a very bright, very smart girl, who liked to be around Whites. She did not like to live in the village. I don't know why. I don't know if she thought she was a White person or what it was. But everyone knows about her. When she was very young she began sleeping with a lot of different men. She was becoming a real whore. Some of the White women felt sorry for her and they tried to get her away from the village and maybe to a school or something, I'm not sure. But the government wouldn't let them take her.

The girl finally got tuberculosis and then leprosy too. She was put in the hospital at Hagen and then she died. She was only about sixteen or seventeen years old when she died, I think. Her father would have nothing to do with her. But I don't know of any other cases like that.

The fashion of intercourse of the Masters is the same as the New Guinean men. The ancestors made men and made women and they are all alike. Black man, White man, both the same as far as screwing goes. I have talked with Baho and some of the other women who have slept with Masters and that is what they say. Baho said the Master didn't kiss her or handle her breasts. He just put his penis in her and pushed and pushed until his water came. Baho says she didn't feel anything. Village men put their hands on our breasts but they don't do anything but squeeze. They like a young, firm, tight breast. If a man squeezes and it's not that way he'll know he has an old woman. Sometimes they squeeze so hard that it hurts.

Big Man Passing

WHEN I WENT TO LIVE IN KAINANTU I DIDN'T KNOW much about our own native medicine. After a while I began to learn about the White man's ways and his medicine. Sometimes I would watch the doctor or doctors' aides at the infirmary. Robaga learned a lot of things too, and he taught me. Taught me to be clean. Told me that we must keep our bodies clean, our clothes clean. That we must wash often. I would tell this to people at the village but they did not pay much attention to this at first.

When Doctor Zigas was here he used to have me help him sometimes. He was a good doctor. He tended to business. He took care of the sick people himself. Didn't just let the doctors' aides do it all, the way some doctors do.

One time he wanted me to take care of a sick woman. She was not at the infirmary but at her house not too far away. He wanted me to take care of her. I did. Sometimes I had to go to see her after dark and I didn't like to go out alone at night. So I asked Doctor Zigas to give me a lantern. He said, "All right. You are helping me, so I will give you a lantern." It was a small kerosene lantern and I have had it for a long time. I still have it. It is the one you bought a new shade for when I came out to Batainabura.

I told you that when I first began learning about White man's ways I would tell the people in the village when I would see them. This was not often at first because I didn't go back to the village very much, and they didn't come into Kainantu as much back in those days as they do now. But by the time I worked for you in 1954, some of the people wanted me to help them. If a woman was going to have a baby she would tell me she wanted me to come and help at the childbirth house. When I did this, I would show them how the doctor did it. How everything should be cleaned. I would wash my hands first and I would tell them that this was the good way to do it. Every time I went to help, the baby was a nice healthy baby. So women like to have me help.

When Bagara had her baby—that was when you were away in the Gadsup village—I went to the childbirth house when they told me. But when I got there she had already had her baby. It came very quickly. So the other women took care of her and it was all right. When I got there I washed the baby for her.

Some women have a lot of trouble when they have babies; some die. The small, one-room childbirth hut is always hot. There is a fire in the middle of the floor. It gets very hot in the room and we all sweat a lot. The mother, especially if she is having trouble, sweats a great deal. Water just runs down her skin, down her front and down her back. We keep her face cool by wiping it with a wet cloth. Keep the sweat out of her eyes. In olden times we used grass but that isn't as good as cloth. Some babies come soon, others take a long time. The mother has to work and work, push and push. Sometimes I have to put my hands in to help pull the baby out. At the infirmary in Kainantu the doctor sometimes cuts the hole in the mother so the baby can come out. We don't do that in the village.

Some women scream a lot because it does hurt so much. The pain may come and go, come and go. Some women hurt so bad that they scream and scream. They let out awful noises. That is one reason the childbirth hut is put so far from the village, so the father won't hear the mother scream in pain.

After the baby comes out, the rope is bitten off and later the end near the baby is cut. We used to do it with a bamboo knife but now a steel knife is used. When I do it I put the knife in the fire first. The doctor says that will clean it. The heat from the fire will make it clean. After the pouch comes out, someone wraps it in leaves and takes it to a nearby stream and puts it in the water. It is no good that a sorcerer get hold of it and work black magic.

I have been married to Robaga a long time. We have had eight children and two of them have died. When I first went to live with Robaga I learned a lot from him. Most of the time he was telling me how to do things. I didn't know anything about how to live in Kainantu. I knew only about life in the village, and Robaga told me many things and taught me many things about living away from the village. He was quite good to me at first, but there have been many times when he has beaten me, when we have had fights.

Many of these fights were just fights; he would be angry with me and we would argue. Sometimes he hit me. Several times, though, he was so mad that he took the case to court at the government office. He didn't do this at first. We didn't have many fights for a long while but we did have some. I think most of the fights have been since I had that affair with Bora. Robaga was very angry about that and since then he gets cross a lot.

Each time that Robaga has taken a case to court he has gone to the doctor first. He goes to the doctor who is his boss, and tells him about the fight. Then he asks the doctor to write a note to the *kiap* for him. We believe that if a Master writes a letter for us the *kiap* will treat us better. But none of the doctors has done this for him so far as I know. They say it is not their business and they can't write a letter to the *kiap* for something like that. So Robaga just goes to the *kiap* and takes the case to court by himself.

Some of the fights have been more serious than others. One time, many years ago—it was when Yebi was young—we were having a fight. Robaga threatened me with an axe. He got very mad. He didn't cut me but he threatened me with the axe. He was angry because I had gone to Haparira for an initiation ceremony. I stayed at Lai's house. Robaga took this case to court but the *kiap* wouldn't settle anything. He said it was our business and we should settle it ourselves.

Another time I remember he again threatened me with an axe. That time he also beat me. He hit me and hit me with his fists but he didn't hit me with the axe. He just threatened to do that. That time, too, he tried to take the case to court but the *kiap* wouldn't do anything about it. Another time I remember well, there were quite a few people at our house. Not the new house I have now, but the one with the thatch roof that we used to live in. We lived in it for many years.

Robaga and I hadn't been having an argument at all. I was just bringing food for people to eat, when he jumped up and hit me. He hit me with his fist and it made a cut on my cheek. He also got a small cut on his hand. He hit me several times and I was quite badly bruised in many places.

My relatives were very angry with him this time. They said that I had not done anything to make him behave this way. They were very angry. They tried to collect pay from him because of this. They said that he was so mean and cruel that he might kill me some time and they wanted to collect the pay now because they knew he wouldn't give them any after I was dead.

This case was taken to court. It was a real case and the *kiap* heard it. But he said that Robaga didn't have to pay my relatives anything for beating me this time. The *kiap* scolded him and told him that he should not be so mean to me, but the beatings did not stop. One time he hit me with a stick. Hit me across the face and I got all bloody. A lot of blood came from my nose as well as from cuts on my face. I was lucky that my nose wasn't broken. But it was very sore where he hit me with the stick.

Not long after this my father, Bano, died. He was an old man. He had not been sick but he had been getting older and older. He was like the other old people. First, the grease began to go from his knees and it was harder and harder for him to walk. After a while he had to use a stick when he walked around although he was not as bad as some of the old people are. And his skin got loose and hung on him. It was flabby and was not firm as it used to be. He did not get blind but we could tell that he could not see as well as he used to. He was like the other old people. Like all of those who are getting old and cannot work the way they used to. He spent a lot of time around his house. He would stay indoors or sit on the ground in front of the house. Sometimes he would lie on his pandanus mat and sleep in the sun. He lived in the upper part of Abiera village and he did not come down into the lower part— almost never.

One day in January 1962 there was a large feast in the lower part of the village and most of the people from up above came down here. Bano didn't come, he stayed all alone in his house. His wife had come down and also Komo and everyone who lived in the house next to Bano's.

While they were gone Bano slept in the sun outside of the house. There was a good sun that day. The door of the house was open and there was a fire inside and some sweet potatoes were roasting in the coals and ashes. After a while, Bano got up and went inside and sat down by the fire. He was hungry and he took some of the sweet potatoes and ate them. He did not know it but while he had been sleeping, a sorcerer had come to the house. He went inside and put poison into one of the sweet potatoes that was cooking on the fire. The poison was meant for Komo, not Bano. But Bano, not knowing about the poison, ate the potato into which it had been put and he ate the poison. This was on Sunday, the day of a big feast in the lower section of the village.

On Tuesday he called for his children living nearby and told them he wanted them to bring him some greens so he could eat them. They brought them and also each one killed a pig and these pigs were cooked in the earth over by Bano's house. After the food had been cooked, Bano took some of the greens and the pig, said some words over it, and put some in a bamboo tube or on a plate for each one of the people he had called to. As he did this, he said, "This one is for Ampe. This one is for Aroba," and so on. That is the way he did it. Ampe told me about this later on. This happened on Tuesday.

On Wednesday, Bano felt all right. On Thursday, too, he was all right, but that day he talked a great deal. Ampe and the others said that he talked almost all the time. He talked a lot more than he usually did. On Friday, Bano did not feel well and he asked Aroba to go to Kainantu to get me. When they came to get me they said that Bano had told them that it was now time to bring the casket that Robaga had made for him quite a while before. Bano had asked Robaga to make the box for him so it would be ready when he died.

We took the box to Abiera and I came out here and brought my children with me. Yebi had just had her first menstruation and I was getting ready to dress her up in her best clothes and jewelry for the feast we were going to give to mark the first menses. But I changed the plans and came right out to Abiera and brought her along with me.

After we arrived here we went directly to Bano's house. All of my children shook hands with him. At first, Hinda was afraid to do it. She was afraid of him. She had not seen him for quite a while and she was afraid of him. He was so old and thin it scared her. But finally she did give him a little handshake. Then he felt of the children's arms and legs.

I shook hands too but I also kissed his nose and face. Then I began to cry. I cried and cried and then Bano began to cry too and we both cried for quite a while. I guess he and I both knew that he would die soon, that his time was almost finished, and so we cried. We stayed with him for several days. We stayed through Monday, Tuesday, Wednesday, and Thursday. On Friday, Bano said, "Is it raining?" And we answered, "Yes, it is raining." Right after that he died. His breath stopped. It was late on Friday when he died.

He knew he was going to die and for a long time he had told us that he didn't want us to wait very long before we buried him. He said we shouldn't mourn for him for a long period. He wanted us to be singing, laughing, and playing again soon after he died. He also told us to bury him soon after he died. He told us this many times. He said, "I'm just like paper. You must bury me quickly. I will be completely gone in a short while."

So, Bano was buried on Sunday. We wailed all day Saturday and all through the night. People came from many places to be at the funeral, for he was a very important man. We cried and cried and cried. You have seen people mourn when someone has died and you know how we do. We cry and cry, wail and wail. Tears stream down our faces. The water gets on our bodies. We cry and cry. Everyone does this but some people wail louder than others. At Abiera, Komo and Koraw are the biggest wailers. They make more noise than all the others. They cry louder. They always do this. It is their way to do it in this fashion. But we all cry hard, although most people do not cry as much as those two men do.

Bano was put in the wooden box and we put many pieces of cloth around him. He was in the box and we would touch him when we wanted to and we would cry and cry. People came from many places to mourn. They would come up to the box and touch him. We were all very sorry that he had died. He was a man of great importance.

Three man dug the hole in the ground for the box. The ground was very hard and there were a lot of rocks in it. The hole was all by itself, there were no other burials near him. Bano had been baptized, so he believed he would go to a good place after he died.

On Sunday we had the feast and it was a big feast. Many pigs were killed and everybody brought a lot of food. It was a very big feast. Many people came to the feast. The oven was fixed in the morning. All the men brought the firewood and put it in the hole. First they cleaned the old rubbish and stones out of the hole. Then they piled the wood in the hole and put the stones on top of the wood. They lit the wood and it burned for quite a while. This heated the stones that fell into the hole as the wood burned up. I think it was about noon when the food was put on the hot stones. It was all covered with leaves, then earth put on it. Then the food cooked.

When the food was nearly done, the wooden box, with Bano's body in it, was carried to the burial place by a few people. After they returned, the food was ready and the oven was opened. There was a lot of food that was served and everyone ate some. There were many pigs and a lot of sweet potatoes, greens, taro, bananas, sugar cane, all kinds of food. This spot on my raincoat is blood from one of the pigs that was killed that day. I have washed it but it won't come out. Now when I see it I think of Bano because the spot is from blood of one of the pigs that was killed when he died.

The next day Robaga took the children back to Kainantu but I stayed on at Abiera. Simi was just a baby so Robaga left him with me; Hinda stayed with me too. That day was Monday and I didn't do much. We were very tired from all the wailing and crying. We just stayed near the house. We slept quite a bit. Slept in the house and also out of doors. There was sun that day and we slept in the sun.

That night I had a dream. In the dream Bano met his mother and she was talking to him. Bano came up to this place in a Jeep; he drove up in a green car. His mother was almost naked. She had only a small pubic covering on. Nothing more. She didn't even have any armlets or any decoration of any kind. She was singing. No special songs, but just singing. She did have good paint on her body. She had put shoe polish on. It is good paint. And she was singing. In the dream my father went to see his mother and she was telling him how good he was. She gave him food and she talked to him a lot. But I don't know what she said. And the songs she sang I don't know. It was just singing.

Tuesday morning I still spent some time sleeping in Bano's house. That day some people came from Kamano territory. They had not come to the funeral. They only heard later that Bano had died and they came on Tuesday. We decided to kill another pig so we could feed the Kamanos. While the men were hunting the pig I slept. My spirit talked to me and told me that the pigs were not where they should be. They were in another area. The men must look elsewhere. When the men came back without a pig because they couldn't find one, I told them where to go to get the pig.

Tuesday night I had another dream. I dreamed that Bano wanted to get a new kind of work. He wanted a different job. He wanted to get some kind of work with a book. In the dream I saw Bano dressed in a white laplap and T-shirt. He went to an office. He went up to this office. It had a black mast. He gave a book to the *kiap* and the *kiap* gave him three bags full of food. The bags were filled with food. Bano put on a policeman's uniform. He put on a laplap, a leather belt, took a rifle, a bayonet, and put on a hat. These were the kind that policemen wear. He told me to take the bags of food. At the time I was holding Haru's second child. It was a baby boy who later died. I was holding him when Bano told me to get the food. I was to get the bags of food. Then Bano went to wash. After that he went to an empty house. It was a policeman's house in Kainantu. It was the only empty house in Kainantu, that's what my spirit told me.

Bano talked to me at this house. I brought the food and the

child. Bano brought a pig and he talked to me. Then I woke up although the dream wasn't finished. I was disgusted because the dream wasn't finished and I woke up. But I knew that my father had gone to a good place. He was not taken to court. He went to a new job. By this time he had gone a long way and I saw him.

On Wednesday I felt much better. I was no longer tired. Thursday I got up and went back to Kainantu. I thought that it was time for me to go. It was no good for me to stay and to keep looking at the place where my father was buried. My father's ghost told me that I should go back. He said it was not good for me to stay and keep looking at the burial place. So I went back to Kainantu.

Bano's wife soon went to live with Ampe. Before he died, Bano told her that she should go to live with Ampe. He said, "Your daughter should take care of you. If you stay here your sons will not look after you very well. But if you go to Kahawta you will be all right. Your daughter will take good care of you. Your sons won't take good care of you but your daughter will." So she followed Bano's advice and went up on the mountain to live with Ampe. Bano had also talked to me and told me to go back to Kainantu. He said it was not good for me to stay at Abiera and think about him all the time. He told me to go back to Kainantu.

Bano's wife didn't put on the usual mourning clothes or decorations. She is an old woman and old women don't have to put on mourning dress as do younger women like Teba. The old women know that their time is coming to an end. They will not marry again. Their time is almost gone and they do not have to put on mourning garb. Only younger women, those who will marry again, have to put on mourning garb. Bano's wife is old and she didn't rip her net bag, or let her hair grow long, or wear any of Bano's gear, as a younger widow does.

Quite a while after I had returned to Kainantu, I had another dream. I saw Bano and he told me to go back to Abiera. Four men had just returned from working on the coast and there would be several big feasts for them. That was the first time I went back after Bano died. I slept at Ika's house. There were three feasts at three earth ovens. One was in the upper village, one in the lower, and one was in between the two.

I didn't go to the upper earth oven near Bano's old house but I did go down below to that part of the village, down along the river by Naro's coffee plot. I washed clothes, I took a bath, and I laid the clothes out to dry. But I didn't go up near the house. Then I returned to Ika's house and Beho brought me three ears of corn that I hung up so they would dry. Later I would cook them and eat them.

This was in April, the fourth month since Bano's death. I came out here on the first day of April. I should have menstruated on the sixth day of April, but I didn't. I knew then that I was going to have another baby.

After I had washed clothes and bathed, I was walking back and I looked up on the mountainside and saw the branches of some trees. They were pointing toward Bano's grave. I felt pulled in that direction and I began to cry. I cried and cried. I walked and walked and walked. After a while I came near Komo's feast and the people there told me I should sit down. There were eight pigs lined up on the ground at that feast and Mago was marking them when I came along. This was just before they were butchered. I cried. Nonke came over and took hold of me. I cried and cried. Komo told me to come sit down and chew betel but I was crying so hard that I couldn't chew it. My liver was about to burst.

I looked over and saw the door of Bano's house. Then I walked up to the grave. I was crying all the time. I cried by the grave and then my crying stopped. I took five shillings out of my purse. I made a small hole in the ground near the cross. I made the hole with my fingers. I wrapped the coins in a piece of paper and I buried them in the hole.

Then I came back down to the lower part of the village and ate food at the feast. I slept at Ika's house and went back to Kainantu in the morning. I didn't ever eat the corn that Beho gave me. I don't know who ate it. I left it tied to a roof pole in Ika's house. I forgot it. So I suppose one of them ate it after it was dried.

I don't know who it was that poisoned Bano, who it was that put the poison in the sweet potato that he ate. That made him die. Komo and Aroba are the men who must find out who did it. I don't know if they know yet or not. They haven't told me. They might know already but I don't know. Women can't find out things like this. Only men know how to tell who makes sorcery.

There are several ways of doing it but I do not know much about it. One of the ways is this. The one who is going to find out who made the poison will have an idea of several people who might be guilty. When he meets one of them he will offer a cigarette or they will share one. He then puts the name of this man on a shell and stands the shell up. If the shell falls down it means the person did not do the sorcery. But if the shell stands up that means the man is guilty. If that happens, the person who is trying to find out who did it will repeat this a second time. He wants to be sure he has found the right person before he retaliates. Another method is to wrap food in leaves, to make several packages of food wrapped in leaves—one for each person or village that might be guilty. The packages are cooked in an earth oven. If one of them comes out only half cooked, that indicates the guilty person or the village where he lives.

This is the method Komo and Aroba used. When they find out who killed Bano they will guard their betel, their lime, and lime gourd and spatula very closely so the culprit can't poison them. They'll guard their tobacco and all the things that they use. They do not want to be poisoned. Komo will have to be very careful because a lot of people think that the sorcerer was trying to kill him, not Bano. They think it was just a mistake that Bano ate the poisoned sweet potato that was really meant for Komo.

I don't know what Komo and Aroba will do to the man when they find out who he is. They haven't told me what they will do. The packet of food that identifies the guilty person is put in the roof of the house. It stays there until the wrong has been avenged. After that the packet will be taken to Bano's grave. They will put it on the grave. Then everything is finished.

I did not put on mourning clothes when Bano died. I did not do it as a village woman would do it. But I did put some of his hair in a new knitted bag. One time, in 1961, I came out here to visit. I visited Bano. I washed his clothes for him. I bathed him. I cut his hair and I shaved his beard. I asked him if I could have some of his hair, the hair from his beard. He said, "Yes. You are my daughter. You can have some hair. You will not use it against me. You can have some." He took some of the hair that I had shaved off his jaw. He made it into a little ball and rolled it back and forth on his thigh. This made it into a stronger piece. He put this in his nose so some of his mucous would be on it, then he gave it to me. I took it and kept it.

After Bano died, I put it in this knitted bag that I got from the Salvation Army Sisters. They put some White man's medicine in these bags and then when people have colds they will give us one. They tell us to breath it into our noses for colds. They gave me one. After the medicine was gone I kept the knit bag and after Bano died, I put his hair in it and I keep it in my little purse. This is like putting the hair into a tiny net pouch and hanging it around my neck. That is what the village women do if they have hair from someone. If that person dies they hang it around their neck. I keep the hair to remember him by.

You know that Bano's house is still standing. The door is locked. There is a padlock on it. The padlock belongs to me. In the house are his plate, his tin box, and other things of his. They are there as he left them. When we see them we can think about him. We have no photo of him but these things of his are the same. When we see them we think of him and cry just as we would if we had a photo. The sugar cane and trees that he planted are still growing too. And when we see them we can think about him. The house will stay there until it rots. But no one can live there. It wouldn't be safe. If we lived there, Bano's ghost might make one of us sick. Children might get sick if we lived in that house or something bad might happen. No, we just leave the house now. It is locked. Some day it will fall down. His things are still inside. But we cannot use it. Komo no longer uses his house which is right next to Bano's.

After Bano died, Komo built a new house and moved there as soon as he could. He was afraid that if he stayed at his old house

Bano's ghost might harm him or his family. Or someone might work sorcery against him. He was afraid something bad would happen, so he moved. He moved out into an open place where there are no trees, to a place where he will be safe. Aruo, Bano's wife, moved away too. She was his first wife and the only one who is still alive. She is very old. You have seen her. She went to live with Ampe at Kahawta right after Bano died. She could not stay here alone.

I have lived in several houses since I have been in Kainantu. I told you what Kainantu was like when I first went there. At that time I lived over near where the Seventh Day Adventist mission is now. There were not many people in Kainantu then. After a while the doctor's office was moved and the infirmary was built where it is now. When you were here in 1954 we lived in the same house we are still in. It is the type that used to be built for us in Kainantu. It had bamboo mats for walls and a thatch roof. There were two rooms inside my house. You have seen it. You know.

Last year the doctor told Robaga he could build us a new house. He gave us a place right on the road. The new house is almost finished. Robaga has built most of it himself. The cook house is still not finished. When it is, we will have a house warming. Robaga told me to ask Jim if he will bring a bottle of gin for the party, as he doesn't like to go to the hotel to buy liquor. When he wants some spirits he has Paulo or someone else get it for him. He doesn't get it often. Just when we have a party. For our party we will have a big earth oven feast. Lots of pigs, rice, canned meat, and sweet potatoes. Lots of food. Some stew, tea, and biscuits too. We will invite a lot of people. It will be a big party.

In 1954 when I worked for you I did make a garden at Abiera. I was living, then, with my own father, Bano, but I used some land that belonged to my mother's brothers, Mando and Beja. The ground I used had once been the land that my mother worked because it had belonged to her father. When she died the land went to her brothers, Mando and Beja.

It was a piece of this ground on which I made a garden when I lived at Abiera in 1954. But I came back to Kainantu before any of the food was ready. I did not get the food from this garden. The food was used by Mando and Beja on whose land the garden was made.

Since then I don't think they've made another garden on it. They have a lot of land so they don't have to use it all. Their sons, Haru and Ika, are lazy and don't work much in the gardens. They let their wives do the work. So their gardens are not large. If these two men worked hard they would make gardens on a lot more of the land that Mando and Beja have and there wouldn't be as much extra land. But I think that any time I go back to Abiera, I can get land from my uncles or my brothers.

I can also use land at Abiera that belonged to my real father, Bano. That was good land too. Komo, the son of one of Bano's brothers, is the oldest son of the lineage. He was in charge of dividing the land as the oldest son usually is. He took most of the land that Bano had at Bentaora and he shared it with Aroba, one of Bano's own offspring. The land that Bano had up on the hillside he gave to Ampe and Barie. He gave some to Kuihu and Hinda too. He also gave some to Bano's mother's relatives. He didn't give me any or any to my other sisters. He told us that we were married to good men and we should follow them. He said we didn't need the land, but that the others did.

Komo is a hard worker. He makes his wives work hard too. Both of them work all the time. Komo doesn't like women who sit around doing nothing. Komo works all the time. Even if he's just sitting down he digs his knees into the ground. He has good gardens and lots of food. He does not waste time.

One time when I went into Kainantu from Abiera, Robaga told me about a big rope of betel nut that Gahabu bought at the market. He bought it, then he gave it to Akro. It was big betel, very big, as big as cucumbers. It was just ripe too. I didn't see it but I heard about it. Then that night I had a dream. My father, Bano, told me that that betel nut belonged to him. He said that he had planted it. That he had watched it grow. He had taken care of the ground. He said that the betel nut belonged to him. He said he had two trees and they belonged to him.

The next day I thought about this dream. I went to Akro's wife, Eto, and told her what I had dreamed. She said, "That betel nut belonged to Indaj." I said, "No, it belonged to papa. He planted it." Eto said, "No, Akro planted it and it belongs to Indaj. Akro planted it on ground that belonged to his father, Indaj."

I was not satisfied. I kept thinking about it. I kept thinking that it really belonged to my father and it was his right to cut it. But Akro kept saying, "It belongs to me," and Akro is a strong man. He is very stubborn. But I am stubborn too and I wanted to get this betel that belonged to my father.

Later, at our house, I kept thinking about this. I went back to Eto's house. I said, "What is it you have done? What did you plant? You planted nothing. Why do you think you can have this betel nut?" I was thinking this, and that is what I said to Eto. I thought I should have the betel nut because it belonged to my father. This is what I thought. I told Eto that.

I said to Eto, "Go get the betel nut and bring it here. I want to see it." Eto got the betel nut and brought it. I looked at it. I said, "I dreamt about this betel. It belongs to me. You can't chew it. I dreamed a song about it. You can't chew it." I talked this way to Eto. I was very stubborn. Finally she gave most of it away and kept the rest. After I talked to her, Eto decided that she should give most of it away. That she and Akro shouldn't chew it all. It didn't really belong to them.

You remember I told you before that I was going to plant coffee while I am here at Abiera this time. You have seen me working down there. That ground once belonged to Bano. It was my father's land. After he died Komo took it. But he has not used it. I did not ask him if I could use it. But he has seen me working there and he has said nothing. So I know it is all right for me to use it. He has plenty of land for his gardens. His gardens are large. His wives are very good workers. He doesn't need the ground that I have taken.

I decided how much land I wanted to have. Then I started to cut the thick grass. I need a lot of help for this. My relatives will help. I also have had some of the children helping me. They can help cut the grass and pull it out. I have paid them in marbles. The other day I paid out one hundred marbles. I gave three marbles to the small children and five marbles to the bigger ones. Afterward I told Boha to go out and play marbles with the children and win them back for me. Then I can use them to pay the children again.

Sixteen women have helped me with the garden. Two men have helped by sitting down nearby and watching! Day before yesterday I had a feast to pay the women. Ika dug the earth oven hole, brought the firewood, and heated the stones for me. We cooked a lot of sweet potatoes on the earth oven. But it rained before the food was fully cooked. We ate it but it wasn't completely done. It is very bad for the food to be half cooked.

Women here in the village are very embarrassed if the food in their earth ovens is not well cooked. It does happen, although not often. This makes women feel very ashamed. You remember at Tata's funeral the food from one of the earth ovens was not fully cooked. The women were very embarrassed about that. But the other day the food would have been all right if it hadn't rained.

So I was not ashamed about the sweet potatoes that were a bit hard. And besides, I had other food that we cooked inside the house; the rain didn't spoil it. There were four pounds of rice, five tins of meat, one squash, some cabbage, onions, and greens. I made a stew of the greens, onions, and cabbage. I also had two stalks of sugar cane that were cut into pieces so people could suck the juice from them. I think the women had plenty to eat. We had fun at the party and I paid them for helping me clear the coffee garden. We still do things this way. It's like long ago—after people helped with a garden, the owners of the garden would give them a feast. The most important garden feasts were given for planting yams.

Ika and Aroba will dig the ditches around the coffee garden and help dig the holes in which the coffee seedlings will be planted. I will get the seedlings from Mayto because he has a good supply and I will not have to pay him for this. I will grow casuarina seedlings in back of our house here and then transplant them by the coffee seedlings so, as they grow, they will shade the coffee trees. It is necessary to have shade for the coffee trees or they will die.

Many people use crotalaria but I am going to use casuarinas. I made the bed for the seedlings. I turned the soil, took out all the weeds, made good soil. Then I put some casuarina branches on the ground so the seeds will fall on it and then grow. Later I will transplant them to the coffee garden. Casuarina is better than crotalaria because the bugs don't get at it as much. Ika and Aroba will do most of the work although others of my brothers and my maternal relatives will help them.

I have already told you that the most important garden feasts are for planting yams. The yams we Tairora grow are very good. We don't grow as many yams as sweet potatoes but in some ways yams are more important. We have stories about why our yams are better than the ones they grow in other places. One of them is about a man and a woman living in the woods near Arogara. The man had a dog. The dog would hunt animals and steal sugar cane for his owner. One day the wife left to find some yams. She went to Agarabi country. The man and the dog stayed behind. The man and the dog waited on the mountain while the woman was gone. They waited and waited. The woman started back from Agarabi territory. She was bringing a lot of yams. One net bag was not enough to hold them all. The dog and the man were watching but they could not see her. She was hidden in a mist. The mist completely enveloped her. They could not see her. They kept looking but they could not see her. As she came back to Arogara, through Tairora territory, they could not see her because she was hidden in the mist.

Each time the woman came up on top of a mountain she looked for the dog and the man. But she could not see them. It was as if they were stones. She could not see the man or the dog. She said, "They must be there somewhere. But I can't see them. Where have they gone? I have come back and now I can't see them." She looked and looked for them but couldn't find them. As she walked around looking for the dog and the man she would drop good yams. Finally she went back to the forest by Arogara. By then she had only second-rate yams to plant there. Since that time, good yams grow only in Tairora country. The yams that grow at Arogara are not very good.

A few days after I left Abiera in December I had this dream. I dreamed that I was back at Abiera. A man had died. I don't know what his name was. Everyone was mourning. They were crying and crying. They didn't go to the garden to get food. A little bird sat on the road. It was a bird that lives in the grassland. A small bird. It was in the middle of the path near Haru's house. Teba said to me, "A man has died and that bird is his ghost. The bird has come and it can't talk." She and I sat down. I saw a car coming along the road. The car came. I waved to it. The car passed us. I don't know who was in the car nor what this dream means.

While I was in Kainantu I had this dream. I went to the water tank to get water. Eto went with me. A Master said to Eto, "You shouldn't get water there now. The tank is empty. Wait until it rains." But I got some water. The Master hadn't come yet. I filled one small bottle with water. That was all there was. After that the Master came and told Eto that she shouldn't get water from the tank. He told her that she should wait. After the tank filled up with water she could get water from the tank.

Robaga has finished our house and cook house now and we will be having the house warming party soon. I will have to buy some pigs for it. I have four pigs here at Abiera. Taria is taking care of two of them, and Komo has the other two. We don't want to use them for the house warming though. We are saving them. In ten months' time Robaga's relatives in the Sepik are going to send a wife for Paulo. We will have a party then and the four pigs are for that. I want to buy other pigs for the house warming.

Last week I went up to Ampe's house at Kahawta. It was the day I left Wanama here with you. I had money that Robaga had given me. I wanted to buy a pig from my sister, Ampe. She has a lot of pigs. I didn't ask her to give me the pig for nothing. I had money to pay for it. But Ampe said, "I don't have any pigs. I can't give you any pigs because I don't have any." But I know that she has a lot of pigs.

When I came back down here I stopped at Bano's old house. I took hold of the padlock. I talked to Bano. I told him that Ampe was not treating me well. I said that Ampe would not give me any pigs. I told Bano all about it. I tapped on the door and held the lock while I told all this. I had his hair in the little pouch—the hair of his that I have told you about. This was in my net bag. I talked to Bano. Told him how Ampe was treating me. Then I came on down. I did this so Bano's spirit would help me. I wanted his ghost to help me and it did.

You remember the other night when we came back from Kainantu, Aroba came to me and told me that Ampe's pigs had gotten into Ioga's garden and ruined much of it. I knew then that Bano had helped me. His spirit had gotten into Ampe's pigs and made them break into Ioga's garden. What I did was not real sorcery. I just asked Bano's spirit to help me out. And that is the way it happened. The spirit made the pigs break into a garden.

Ampe and Ioga had a big fight. Ampe had to kill three pigs to settle it all. She had a big earth oven feast. But I didn't go to it. A lot of people from here went up. I didn't go. One man who came was Gamu. He is a brother of mine. He lives at Ehubajra but goes to Ontabura a lot to be with his wife's family. When he came from Ontabura on his way to Ampe's feast, he stopped here. He offered to kill a pig for my house warming, said he could do it tomorrow. He said that his father had done many things for my maternal kin and he would do things for me. He would kill a pig. But I told him to wait. I told him the house warming will be in two weeks. He can kill the pig then. Since he can kill only one pig, I must find still more.

While I was in Kainantu this past weekend I worked quite hard. I washed clothes on Friday. Had a lot of them to do. My clothes and those of Wanama, Anto, and Simi from here, as well as the clothes of Robaga, Paulo, and Hinda in Kainantu. It took me all day to do it. I carried all of the clothes down to the river. There were two net bags full of them. No one else was there so I had the best rocks to work on. These rocks are large and flat and good for washing clothes. Some of the rocks are not as smooth and flat as others. This time I had the best ones. I wet all the clothes, then one by one I put them on the rock and rubbed soap on them. I bought a lot of soap at the trade store. When a blouse was soapy, I picked it up and beat it against the rock. Then I rinsed the soap out by swishing it back and forth in the part of the river that was fast flowing. It took a long time to wash all the clothes.

On Saturday I spent most of the day in the garden. I tied up the sugar cane and took care of other things too. I came back here on Sunday and Robaga walked out here with me. He returned to Kainantu in the late afternoon. He told me to get my money back for the pig. I paid five pounds for a pig that they got for me at Noreikora. It was small and not worth more than three pounds. I couldn't get anyone to take it back to Noreikora so Kea said he would buy it, keep it, and fatten it up. But he hasn't paid me.

Robaga says I should get my money back. We can get a pig for ten pounds at another village. It will be a big pig. We can't have the party now anyway. The doctor is going away and wants some work done on his house. He has given Robaga a lot of extra work to do. So Robaga has to work hard all the time now. After that, we can have our house warming. Then we can get a pig.

Into a Widening World

OUR NEW HOUSE IS VERY NICE. ROBAGA BUILT IT. HE also made the chairs, tables, and beds. We have two bedrooms and another room and a small porch. There are two beds in each bedroom. Robaga has one bedroom. I have the other. Simi, Anto, and Hinda sleep in the front room with Robaga. Yebi sleeps there when she is home from school. Simi and Anto sleep in the bed with Robaga when Hinda and Yebi are there.

Hinda doesn't like to sleep with anybody. Nor does she like to share her things with anyone else. Even her bed and blanket she doesn't want to share with anyone. But when Yebi is home from school she sleeps with Hinda.

Wanama sleeps with me. Sometimes when I sleep on my back she crawls up and lies on my chest. Paulo's bed is in my room and that is where he sleeps. Robaga keeps all of his things in his room and I keep my things in my room. Robaga has a lot of things but I don't.

We spend a lot of time in the cook house. It is in back of the house. It has a cement floor, a slab on the ground, not a raised wooden floor like the house. When people come we usually sit on the floor around the fire in the cook house and talk. We have tea and I give food to people when they come. Many Tairora from Abiera, Ontabura, and Haparira come to visit us. When they come to Kainantu they come to our house. I think more people come to our house than to Eto's. Many people come and eat our food. Most of them will reciprocate. They bring food to us. Bring some pork if they have killed a pig.

But some people, like Amuri and Haru, come all the time, eat our food, and they never bring us anything. All they think about is playing cards and gambling. They don't work hard. Their wives do

143

all the work. The two men are lazy. They never bring us any food or anything. They come to see us more than most people do, too.

I was very cross with them when they wouldn't go to Noreikora to get the pig for our house warming. They were picking coffee for Amata. When they got paid for that they just played more cards, gambled at Lucky. They should have gone to get the pig for me. I have given them so much food in Kainantu. And Haru is my brother. Amuri is too, but not as close.

Many people came to our party. When you drove me into Kainantu on Thursday afternoon everyone saw us coming. Robaga and everyone else was pleased with the amount of food we brought. There was a lot of all kinds of food that we brought from the village. Sweet potatoes, sugar cane, bananas, and greens. Eleven of my friends and relatives all gave a lot of food. Then at Haparira we picked up firewood and sugar cane. When we got to Kainantu we unloaded it all. Then there was a lot of work to do but I was glad to learn that Paulo and Mayto had prepared the two earth ovens. There was one for the pig and one for the goat.

Saturday many people arrived for the party. They came from Abiera, Borawta, Tongera, Ontabura, and Haparira. A lot of people came. We had a tarpaulin hung up in the backyard so people could sit under it. It was near the earth ovens. Some people came into the cook house and some into the house. Most of them stayed outside.

We all helped fill the ovens. Inside the cook house I boiled rice and greens. I made soup and people ate that too. After the ovens were opened we cut the pig and goat and divided the meat and the other food and then most people went home.

Eto helped me most with this but there were others who helped too. Eto knows how to cook and she helped me. For this party mostly people from the villages came. The people that live in Kainantu don't like people from the villages. Most of the New Guineans that live in Kainantu come from other areas: from the coast, from Hagen, from Chimbu, from Wabag. They come from all over. Not many are from the Tairora area. So at this party we had people from the villages and just a few from Kainantu. The style of the Kainantu people is different. This party was in our old fashion. People from the villages brought a lot of food. They all helped us with it. Robaga bought the pig and goat. Then we divided up the food.

A party with just Kainantu people is different. A man and woman give the party all by themselves. They give the food. The other people don't help them. This fashion of helping is that of the village people. Village people think the other way is very bad. They think the way the people in Kainantu give parties is not right. As Ihube told you, "They are like pigs. They don't work hard for your party. They just come and eat. They're like pigs."

The night after we first came out to Batainabura I had a dream. I dreamed that you had given me five tins of fish. You said, *"Ma!"* and I looked and you were holding five tins of fish out to give to me. I took them. That is all I dreamed. In the morning I got up and I looked by my pillow. I looked and looked. I stretched my neck and looked all round. But didn't see the tins of fish. I said to Ihube and Boha, "Have you seen my tins of fish?" They said, "No." I said, "Missis gave me five tins of fish." Then I realized that I must have been dreaming about it. The fish were not with my things and Boha and Ihube hadn't seen them either.

The night after we went to the cave, the time you and Jim and Ihube, Ika, Abu, and I went to that cave, I dreamed this. There was a line of policemen along the road. There were nine of them. The corporal made ten. The sergeant made eleven. There were eleven police walking along the road. I saw them. I was standing on the road and they came along. The boss of all of them was cross with me. He stood close to me and he bawled me out. "What is it you want to say to us?" The sergeant was standing behind. Just the corporal talked. "What is it you want? What do you want to say that made you stop us?" I said, "No good that I stopped you." That's what I was thinking. And I went on my way. I went around them. I went on along the road. The men stopped going in their direction and they followed me. The corporal said, "Missis has gone but she belongs up here." That's what he said to me. My spirit replied, "You can't talk that way to me. I know better than you. I am not a missis and you shouldn't talk that way to me. I am the only one here that is blocking your path." The corporal said to me "Do you want to go to court? If you do, all right, we can take you to court." He talked this way.

Then I woke up. The dream ended. I thought about the dream and this is what I think. While we were going to the cave we walked along the river. We saw a bird on a rock. I was near the rock and Ika and Ihube wanted to catch the bird. They got a stick to throw at it. I was in the way. I was standing there near the rock the bird was on. I was in their way for throwing the stick at the bird. And they wanted to catch the bird. They talked to each other. One was going to shoo the bird away and the other would throw the stick. I was watching them and I was in their way. Because of this, they threw the stick crooked the first time. After that they moved so I wasn't in the way. Then they caught the bird.

Not long ago the government began to talk about the election.[9] We all thought, "What is this election? What is it all about? What do we do? What does it mean for us?" We didn't know about election. It was the same everywhere. The *kiap*s would have everyone come together at one place. Then they would tell people what the election was. They told us first in Kainantu. Then they went out to all the villages. They told us all about it. They said that we would choose some men. These men would go to Port Moresby and make the laws for us. The *kiap*s said we would choose who would go. They wanted some local men to go to Moresby. We would say which ones would go. The *kiap*s went to all the places to give this talk. They wanted everyone to know about this.

Akro was one of the New Guineans who wanted to go to Moresby to make the laws. He walked around to many villages. He told all the people that he was the one they should send. He thought all the Tairora would vote for him. I think most of them did. At first I thought he was the best one. Later, when I learned more about it, I thought the Kamano man was best. Better than the Agarabi or the Gadsup. Better than Akro.

Akro was anxious to go to Port Moresby. He thought he should go there. But Eto, his wife, did not want him to go. She said that if he went to Moresby she would not go with him. She said she

Young girls feasting after emerging from first menses seclusion.
The girl seated in the center of the front row is wearing
new skirts, new arm bands, and a new necklace.

Above: Smoke from an outdoor fire is enjoyed,
especially on cool highland days.

Top right: Group with newly acquired produce.

Bottom right: The polling place where Anyan and other Tairora
voted in the first election to be held in Papua New Guinea.
Built especially for the occasion, it was a thatched roof,
open sided shelter, embellished with a variety of plants.

Male initiate wearing sporran and bark arm decoration,
shell necklace, head band, and polished stone ornament
in the hole pierced through his nasal septum.

A well dressed man of yesteryear wears arm bands,
a net bag slung around his neck, pig tusks in the hole
pierced through his nasal septum, and head gear
of cowrie shells and cassowary feathers.

A woman's lips and nose show the effects of yaws.
In her case, yaws was arrested before it became crippling.

Anyan's and Robaga's old house in Kainantu,
shortly before it was abandoned.

Anyan's new house, built in 1964 by her husband Robaga,
consists of a living room and two bedrooms on piles.
Just visible at the rear are a wall and roof of the cookhouse,
a separate structure erected on a cement slab.
During the cooler winter months, the family
spends much time around the open fire
in this building.

would divorce him if he went. I don't think she would though. But she might not go to Moresby with him.

Besides the New Guineans, three Australians wanted to win the election. They went to a lot of villages to talk to the people. They told them what they would do for the people here. They told them what they thought. One of the Australians tried to teach people about the election. But they all talked about how the people would vote. They would send some of these men to Moresby. The men would make new laws for us. They would build more roads, give us machines, do many things for us. All these men went around talking about the election. They said that New Guinea must have these men in Moresby who would make the laws.

Akro told Holloway that it is time the locals are on top of things here in New Guinea. The Australians have been in control for a long time here and the New Guineans under them. Now it is time for them to take control and the Australians to be under them. This is what Akro said.

The Aiyuras also told the *kiap* this. They told the *kiap* they don't care if he leaves New Guinea or not. The Aiyuras say they are here on this land. They have always been here. They will always stay here. One time the Aiyuras told the *kiap* that if he wanted to have court for them he must come to Aiyura. So the *kiap* went to Aiyura for court. He asked the Aiyuras if they wanted the Australians to leave. The Aiyuras said they didn't care. It was all right if they did or all right if they stayed. But they think like Akro. They think the Australians should now let go of control and New Guineans should be on top.

I had this dream before the election took place. I saw two chickens of mine. One of them, a yellowish brown one was inside the house. The other, a black one, was outside. The one inside had laid an egg and was sitting on it. I saw it. My other chickens were asleep in the garden. I walked around and looked at them. Then Nomi's wife and daughter came along. They had some chickens with them. After a while I saw a black chicken of theirs sleeping above my yellow-brown chicken. Their chicken was on top. Mine was down below. Their black one was above my brown one. The wing of the chicken on top fluttered and I saw it. My chicken was sleeping down below. I said to Nomi's wife, "I saw my chicken and it was sleeping under your chicken." I said this to her.

Then I saw five jail inmates. They had killed a dog of Holloway's. The dog was dead and had bruised skin. There were red and black marks on him. They had killed the dog. I saw it. I said, "You have killed Holloway's dog." They didn't say anything. The five were singeing the hair of the dog and they wanted to cut it up. I saw the jailees and I said, "That is Holloway's dog. You can't cut it up." They said, "We killed it and we can cut him up. No good someone else cuts him up. We will cut him." I was watching them and they butchered it. It was Holloway's dog and our dog was down below. Then the dream ended.

The next morning I told Ihube and Boha about my dream. I wondered what it meant. Did it mean that after the election the Agarabi would be on top and the Tairora down below? We Tairora would sleep underneath and the Agarabi would be on top? I didn't know so I asked Ihube and Boha. Boha and Ihube said they didn't think so. I think so. But they said, "After the election comes up we can know the answer." After everyone has voted we can know about this. If they all go against Mr. Holloway, we will win. I don't think it will happen. But I really don't know for sure.

For a long while I thought that I would vote for a man from the Sepik. I was married to a Sepik man and I thought I would vote for a man from his area. This is what I thought. I knew I would vote for Kainantu too. I had lived in this area always. I knew I would vote for someone from here. But I thought I would vote for the Sepik man too. I was going to ask Robaga which Sepik man I should vote for. But then I learned that I couldn't vote for a Sepik. I could only vote for men from the Kainantu area.

I was living at Batainabura when the voting took place. I thought maybe I could not vote there. Only in Kainantu. I was not too unhappy about it. I was a bit scared to vote. There was plenty of talk going around about people getting sick from voting. Some people in Gadsup got sick from voting. Got really sick from it. And we heard about many other people who got sick from voting. A wind would blow over them when they voted and they would get very sick. I did not want to get sick and I was afraid to vote. But I didn't take the medicine that some of the people at Batainabura took. They took it just before they went to vote. A lot of them ate aromatic bark. They had an earth oven feast. Spat a mixture of aromatic bark on the food and ate it. They rubbed pig grease on their bodies. I didn't do this.

Another thing that was done at Batainabura was this. A few days before the election, the head man told all the women to come to his house one night. He told all the women to come and many did. But not all of them went there. When they got there he told them that if they didn't want to get sick when they voted, they must tell him all the bad things they had done. They must tell him about all the affairs they had had with other men. He said they should tell him everything bad if they didn't want to get sick when they voted. Some of them did tell him. But some of them wouldn't tell him. Many of them had not been bad and they told him so. But he wanted to know about affairs they had had a long time ago. With the older women he wanted to know about them when they were younger. He said they all must tell him about these affairs with men if they didn't want to get sick.

Some of the men heard about this and they were very angry. They were afraid that the women would tell on them. Then their wives or the husbands of the women with whom they had slept would be mad. They were very angry. Some of them tried to listen through the walls of the head man's house. Some even called to their girl friends to come out of the house. They were very angry. But I don't think they did anything to the head man. I don't think they could. But they were very angry. A lot of women didn't like it either. Some of them didn't believe what the head man said about their getting sick. They didn't tell anything.

As you know, the Tairora wanted Akro to win. The people at Abiera had a big dance there. They had plenty of food, lots of food. People came from all over. The Ontabura and Haparira people came to help and they had some earth ovens. But the dance arbor was built at Abiera and most of the ovens were made by the

Abierans. Most of the food came from there too. People came from all over to the dance. It was a big dance.

Some Australians came too. Some of them came to the dance. Some came the next day to talk to all the people that had come there from all over the region. It was a big dance; the biggest I have seen. And the Abiera people did it for Akro. They thought that this would make him win in the election.

I was living at Batainabura at the time of the election. The day we voted, we all went down to the voting place near Noreikora. The *kiap* came the night before. The people had built a house for voting. The *kiap* did not think it was good enough and they did not have enough food for him. He got very angry with them. He also got cross with some of the Batainaburans who were there helping.

Then on the day to vote, we all went down there. There were a lot of people from a large area. I didn't stay with the Batainaburans all the time. I knew the policemen who were with the *kiap*. I have known them for a long time in Kainantu. I had not seen them for quite a while and I talked to them a lot. I didn't just sit and wait with the Batainaburans although I went down there with them. But I voted when they did. I went in to vote when the Batainaburans went in.

We went in one at a time. The clerk read all the names on the paper and I told him which ones to mark. Then he gave me the paper and I put it in the red box. The red metal box was locked but there was a hole in the top that we could put the paper in. Then I went out. I was afraid when I did it but nothing has happened to me since then.

After the voting was all over most of the people went home. But Ihube, Abu, and I stayed to play Lucky. We had been playing before the voting stopped. The *kiap* came over and looked at us to see if we were using money. But we weren't. So he didn't say anything to us. Ihube and Abu and I stayed after the others went home, and we played Lucky for quite a while.

Akro did not win the election. Holloway won. Akro is very angry that he didn't win and all the Abiera people do not know why he didn't. They worked so hard to make him win. But Holloway won. He beat all of the New Guineans who wanted to go to Moresby to make the laws. Akro was mad about it. But I think he feels all right now. At first he was so angry he didn't want to continue as interpreter for the *kiap*. He has been the Tairora interpreter for many years.

When I first went to Kainantu I interpreted for the *kiap*. There wasn't too much to do then. Later Akro went to work for them and a few years ago they got a second Tairora interpreter because there are so many Tairora going into Kainantu. Akro threatened to stop being the interpreter, but he didn't carry it out. He is still the Tairora interpreter.

Yesterday I was walking up on the big road. I saw two men coming from Tompena. I could see them walking this way. When they came near I could see that they had a big snake. It was a great big one. They bought it at Tompena for seven shillings. Someone caught it in the forest near Akuna. It was a very long snake. When they came near me I saw how big it was. I was frightened. I jumped over to the side of the road and fell in the ditch.

I turned my ankle and hurt it badly. Today I have to walk with a stick. I have been hitting my ankle and leg with nettles. This will help cure it. But it still hurts very much. It is black and blue and very swollen. I bandaged it with the cloth you gave me. I put some nettles on the ankle. Then I put the bandage around that. The ankle and leg hurt a lot. But I don't think I will have it bled. I'm not sure that will help.

I was very frightened by the snake. In our country we don't have snakes. Once in a while, a small one. But over at Akuna in Gadsup country there are a lot of snakes. Great big ones. There are a few here in the Batainabura bush too. I am very much afraid of snakes. This was a great big one. Very long. One of the longest snakes I have ever seen.

When we left Abiera for Batainabura most of the holes had been dug in my coffee garden but nothing had been planted in them, although Ika had planted coffee beans so we could have seedlings to plant. Last weekend I went back to Abiera to plant the seedlings but the ground was too wet for planting. The seedlings are ready but we could not plant. I told Ika he should put a roof over the seedlings so they don't get wilted by the sun. I was very cross with people because my garden is all full of weeds and grass again. I bawled them out.

My maternal kin should have kept the weeds out of the garden while I was at Batainabura. But they didn't. They just let the weeds grow. I was very cross with them. I said, "Why haven't you taken care of my garden? I went to Batainabura and you should have taken care of my garden. You owe it to me to help with my garden. After a while I will return some favors to you. Why are you so lazy? Look at that garden. It is full of weeds. I worked hard to clear that garden. You should have taken care of it for me." But I couldn't plant that day. After you go back to America I will go out there again. Then I can plant the coffee trees.

Robaga and I have had other bad fights that I have not told you about. One time I had been working hard for several days. I washed clothes, cooked, cleaned the house, and did some knitting. I worked hard.

On a couple of evenings I went to a neighbor's house to watch some of the other women play Lucky. There are some women at the station that like to play Lucky. Some of them play a great deal and they gamble quite a bit. The *kiap* doesn't want people to gamble and play Lucky but some of them do. So, I would watch them. Those times I did not play, I just watched. I was not far from my house, just next door. Hinda was with me and from time to time I would send her back to the house to see if the baby was all right. She was sleeping and she did not need me.

Robaga was angry with me for having gone to watch the women the first time. The next time I went I told the women what Robaga had said and they laughed at him. They think he is silly to be so stubborn against my playing Lucky. Paulo was outside and he heard the women laughing at Robaga and joking about him. So he wrote a note and had Simi take it to Robaga. He told Robaga what the women said and that they had laughed at him. When Robaga came home that night he was very angry. He yelled at me. He threatened me. Said I should not even go to watch the Lucky game. He grabbed a piece of firewood and threatened to hit me. I grabbed another stick and told him he'd better not hit me. We argued a lot and threatened to hit each other. Again, he accused me of having an affair with Bora. He always does this when he gets mad at me. I am sick and tired of his bringing it up. The matter was closed years ago, in 1954. I have had nothing to do with Bora since then and it makes me sick to have Robaga bringing it up all the time.

He also tells me over and over that when my father, Bano, died, he, Robaga, dug the hole and nailed the box. He didn't really dig the hole but by saying that he means that he helped to make the payments at the time of my father's funeral. And he did make the coffin for him. We didn't hit each other during this fight and after a while we cooled off. But in a couple of days we argued again and we kept on having arguments and fights.

One time Robaga told me that he was going to take me to court again. I was very angry then and I told him that I had only one thing to tell the *kiap*. If Robaga took me to court I would tell the *kiap* that I was through with Robaga. I was ready to leave him any time. I had had enough of him and his jealousy. Although he once played Lucky, he doesn't now and he thinks no one else should. A long time ago I used to play quite a bit of Lucky, but the last few years I haven't. I still like to watch other people play, though, and I don't see anything wrong with that. I have played a few times in the last year but not very much.

One time Robaga gave two shillings to Paulo and told him to give them to Simi. I got them away from Simi and played Lucky with them. I lost them and couldn't return the two shillings until later. Another time Paulo let me have two shillings. That time I played Lucky and I won six shillings so I ended up with eight. The women often ask me to play because they know I like to. But I don't do it very often. They tease me a lot because of the way my husband acts. They laugh at Robaga because he feels so strongly against Lucky.

One of the most avid players among my friends in Kainantu is my good friend, Eto. She plays a lot. Her husband gets mad at her sometimes because she plays so much, but he doesn't tell her that she should never play. They have argued a couple of times and he has grabbed her and choked her a bit, but that is all. I don't think he hit her over Lucky, just choked her.

We all think Robaga is wrong. Sometimes I say to him, "What is the matter with you? I cook for you. I have had plenty of children for you. I take good care of you. But you are not good to me. Other women cook for their husbands, give them food, and are good to them. And the husbands appreciate it and give their wives some money so they can play Lucky. Why don't you behave that way? Why don't you act like other men and be good to me?"

But it doesn't do any good. He is very stubborn about it. Paulo feels the same way and always helps his father. The last time I played Lucky, the time I lost the two shillings, Paulo saw us. He called out to the police master to come and arrest us. It was Paulo who tried to have us arrested. But the police master didn't come. Paulo told on us though.

I have told Robaga that if he takes me to court again I will leave him. I've had enough. Even though I have to give up the children, I won't live with him any longer. I could keep Wanama for a while, but the others could go with their father if they wanted to. The *kiap* says that if a woman leaves her husband the man can keep the children. On the other hand, if a man sends his wife away, she may take the children with her if they want to go.

If Robaga doesn't take me to court I will stay with him but if he goes to court again I'm through with him. I'll go back to Abiera to live. I won't go to Batainabura nor will I marry Bora. I would just go to Abiera and live there. I wouldn't be in a hurry to get married again. I have born Robaga many children. I have made his lineage a strong one. It is large and strong and I have made it that way. But I have had enough and I won't stay with him longer if he takes me to court again.

You remember I told you about the election. How we all went from Batainabura to Noreikora to vote. While we were waiting to vote I didn't sit with the Batainaburans. I knew the policemen and the other people who were with the *kiap* and I talked to them. After we had voted, Ihube, Abu, and I played cards with some of the men who were with the *kiap*. We played in a small building out in back of the cook house that belongs with the *kiap* house, the house where the *kiap* stays when he is taking the census and holding court. You remember I told you that the *kiap* came over and watched us. He wanted to see if we were gambling. But we weren't so he didn't stop our playing. After you and all the other Batainaburans left, Ihube, Abu, and I stayed on and played cards.

When we walked back to Batainabura that evening, Abu told me that he liked me a lot. He said that he thought about me all the time and he wanted to have an affair with me. This is the first time that he told me this. But I guess his wife, Bamba, has thought about it for quite a while. You know about the two fights they have had because Abu spends time with Ihube, Boha, and me instead of helping Bamba in the garden.

At first Bamba thought that I was unmarried and looking for a husband and she was jealous of me. But I told her that I am married and have several children. She knows that. She is a very jealous woman and is always nagging Abu about something. Now that Abu's first wife is dead and Bamba is his only wife she is very jealous of him. But she has had affairs with plenty of men herself. Abu has been good to all of us from Abiera. He brings us a lot of food. And he does like to come to our house to sit around and talk. But it was just when we came back from voting that he told me how much he liked me.

One afternoon, a week or two later, after you and I returned to Batainabura—you had been at Ukarumpa and I had been at Kainantu—Ihube and I went down to the river to bathe. Two other women were there so I bathed with them and Ihube waited up on the path while we women took our baths and washed our clothes. After we were through we walked up the hill to the path so Ihube could come down and take his bath. Abu had come and was waiting with Ihube. The two of them went down to the river to bathe and we waited for them.

While we were waiting I made a cigarette. I took a piece of newspaper, tore it to the right size, very long, and softened it between my fingers. Then I cut some rope tobacco in it, rolled it up, and licked the paper along the edge so it would stick.

Ihube left his cloth sack and Abu left his net bag lying on the ground near where we were sitting. While they were gone I took his pomade out of Abu's net bag and put some on my hair as I combed it. After the two men came back, Abu knew what I had done and he pretended to be cross with me but he also joked about it. I know he was really happy that I had used something that belonged to him. Happy because I had used a personal article of his. He asked me why I had taken it and I said that I needed some for my hair, that was all. I told him that I didn't think he would care if I used a little of it.

We started up the hill, all five of us, and Abu asked me if it were true that I had left Robaga for good. I said, "No. We had a big fight last week and we are still very angry with each other. But I haven't left him." Then Abu said, "All right. If you do leave him I want to marry you, that's all."

As we walked along I was smoking the cigarette I had made. When I'd had enough I handed it to Ihube so he could smoke it. After he had finished he handed it to Abu who kept it and smoked it until it was all gone. Ihube was walking by me then and he remarked about Abu's smoking up my cigarette completely. But I told him that it was all right because I had used his pomade. When we got near the top of the mountain, a friend gave me some sweet potatoes and I wrapped them up in my towel. Abu carried them on up to our house for me. He and Ihube and I returned to the house together.

Later Ihube told me that I shouldn't let Abu flatter me and try to get me to have an affair with him. He said that he, Ihube, as my brother, was responsible for me here. It was up to him and Boha, my brothers, to see that I didn't do anything wrong. He told me that he would hit me if I did anything wrong. He probably would too, because a brother is supposed to take care of his sister, and if a woman misbehaves the brother gets angry and hits her. When I had that affair with Bora, Ika gave me a good beating.

Ihube looks after me well here at Batainabura. If he goes out at night to play Lucky or just to walk around to visit some of the people, he locks the door of the house and takes the key. Sometimes he locks both Boha and me in, and once I was there alone when he locked me in. He is very protective of me and he is insistent that I do not get into any trouble here.

I have told Abu's wife, Bamba, many times, that I am not interested in getting a husband here, that I am married and have not left my husband. I tell her that I am not going with Abu. My husband has money and he is able to buy me a lot of things with it. I asked Bamba if her husband can do that. Bamba knows that Abu doesn't have much money and could not buy many things. I tell her that I could never live at Batainabura. Abiera would be all right, but Batainabura is too rural to suit me.

Robaga and I are still having problems. We went to court on Monday morning. Robaga complained to the *kiap* that I played Lucky. He also complained that I hadn't come back to take care of him and the children when they were sick a couple of months ago. But how could I? I didn't know they were sick until they were well again. I told the *kiap* that I was through with Robaga, that I'd had enough of his beatings and that I wanted to leave him. I told him how he treated me and that I was afraid to stay with him any longer. I told the *kiap* how he threatened me with an axe, as well as about all the times he beat me.

The *kiap* told Robaga that he shouldn't treat his wife that way. He said that a man can't treat his wife that way and expect her to want to stay with him. The *kiap* told Robaga that he had been in Kainantu for over twenty-five years and that he and I had been married for twenty years and that we should be able to get along together all right. The *kiap* talked to us like this for a while. Then he told us to go home, to sleep the night, and to come back on Tuesday if we still wanted the case in court.

Tuesday morning we went back. The *kiap* asked Robaga if he still wanted to make his complaint against me. Robaga didn't answer. The *kiap* asked him again. Robaga didn't say anything. The *kiap* pounded his fist on the table and asked Robaga again if he had anything to say. He asked why he had come if he didn't have anything to say. Then the *kiap* asked me if I had changed my mind and I said, "No. I still want a divorce."

Then the *kiap* told me that because Robaga wouldn't say anything that I had won something because evidently Robaga didn't want to divorce me or even to bring the case to court now. But I still wanted a divorce and that is what I told the *kiap*. So he told us to come back again on Wednesday morning and to bring our children with us.

On Wednesday morning we all went over to the office. Robaga and I along with Paulo, Hinda, Anto, Simi, and Wanama. The *kiap* said to Paulo, "How old are you?" Paulo said, "I am eighteen." Then the *kiap* asked him if he wanted to stay with Robaga or me. He said he wanted to stay with Robaga. Then the *kiap* said to Hinda, "How old are you?" Hinda said, "I am ten." Then he asked Anto how old she was and she told him she was seven. The *kiap* asked Hinda and Anto if they wanted to stay with Robaga or me and they both said they would stay with Robaga.

Then the *kiap* asked Simi how old he was. But Simi didn't answer. He just ran around the room and smiled. He ran around the *kiap*, too. He didn't stay in one place, just kept running around the room. Then the *kiap* said that Simi and Wanama were too young to know where they wanted to stay and that they needed their mother.

I told the *kiap* that I could keep them for a while and that when they were old enough to decide, I could bring them back to Robaga if they wanted to stay with him. I also told the *kiap* about Yebi. I told him that she is fifteen and that she goes to school in Lae. I didn't tell the *kiap*, but I think Yebi would want to stay with me. Yebi likes Kainantu and she likes Abiera. She has told me several times that she doesn't like Robaga's place, the Sepik area that she has visited. She likes Kainantu and the highlands best. She doesn't want to go to the Sepik and she has told Paulo that he can pay for a wife there, that she doesn't want to go in exchange. Paulo doesn't want to marry a girl from around here in the highlands. He wants to marry a girl from the coast. But Yebi has told him that she doesn't want to go in exchange, so he should pay for his wife if he gets one from there.

Yebi likes Nomi's son. Nomi adopted him from a Kamano when he was about a year old. Yebi and Nomi's son were in school together in Kainantu. He goes to school in Goroka now and she goes to school in Lae. They have exchanged photographs and they write letters to each other. Yebi also writes letters to Nomi and his wife. So I think Yebi will stay with me. The others can go with their father. It is enough if I have one child.

The other children have chosen their father over me. They think they will not miss me so I will not miss them either. If I have one child that is enough. If any one of them changes his mind and wants to come back to me after a while that is all right. I would take him back. But now they all say they want to go with the father and that is all right with me. I will have Simi and Wanama for a while and then we can see.

The afternoon after we went to court with the children, Oaj died. So on Thursday I went to Aiyura for the funeral. We spent two nights there. I went back to Kainantu on Saturday. After I got back I saw Akro. He had been down in South Tairora country directing the building of some bridges. He had just come back and had just heard about Robaga and me. He talked to me for quite a while. He told me that I should not leave Robaga. That it would be better if I would stay with him. He said it was not good for me to leave the children. He talked quite a while and he kept telling me this. So I will stay with Robaga and the children.

My Two Lives

NOW, WHILE I AM SPENDING PART OF THE TIME IN THE VIL-
lage, Wanama wants to be with me all of the time. Even
though other women want to take care of her, she does
not like to go with them. She is different from the children here in
the village. Village children always have some relatives around.
There is always a mother, or a father, aunts, uncles, grandparents,
brothers, and sisters. Not just one father or mother, but several. All
will help to take care of the child. They like to do it. So village
children are used to having many different people take care of
them. Different people hold a child, play with it, even suckle it.
Sometimes if an older child wants to suckle at its mother's breast
and the mother is busy, another woman can offer hers. Even an old
woman. The child doesn't expect to get milk but just likes to suck.
Wanama is not like that. She is used to getting milk from my breasts
and she cries if an older woman wants her to suck at her breast.

When a village child is handed to another person, the mother
will say to it, "This is your grandmother," or "This is your mother's
brother," or "This is your father's sister." In this way the child
knows what to call all of these people. He learns what relationship
they are to him. In the village if a mother goes to the garden she
can leave her child with someone who is staying in the village. If it
is a very young baby she will probably always take it with her, but
when it is older she can leave it with someone in the village. If a
child's mother and father are from the same village, the child has
many, many relatives to help take care of it. Both mother's and
father's relatives can help. If the mother comes from far away,
there are not so many relatives to take care of the child.

It was very bad to leave a child alone in the village. Very bad.
And it was almost never done. There is a story about this. One day

a mother left her child at home alone. She went to the garden to work. Wild cat came to the house and asked the child, "Where is your mother?" The child said, "Mother has gone to the garden to get greens." Wild cat stayed. He said, "I don't want you to be here alone. I came to be with you." Then he screwed the girl. After that he got ashes from the fire, rubbed the girl's skin, and went away. Each day he would come back. He would ask the girl the same thing. He would do the same thing. One day the girl's mother did not really go to the garden. She went into the other room. She covered herself with a pandanus mat and kept very quiet. She hid and waited and waited. Wild cat came. "Where has your mother gone?" The child answered the same as usual. Wild cat tried to fuck the girl. The mother saw him. She was very angry. She jumped up and grabbed wild cat. She threw him on the fire and he was badly burned. Since then, wild cats have black, white, and brown colors mixed up on them.

In the villages it was common to leave children with someone while the mother and father went to the gardens to work. But one had to be sure the person would do a good job of looking after the children. We have a story that says how important this is. How we should not leave a child with someone who won't do a good job of taking care of it. A man and a woman left their children in the village with an old woman. The old woman was almost blind. The man and woman went to their work. While they were gone, the wind blew down a wooden plank. It hit the children and knocked them over. They were knocked down. After a while the mother came back. She said to the old woman, "Get the children and bring them to me. They can nurse. My breasts are full and they are too tight." The old woman replied, "I don't see well. I have not been able to watch the children. I wonder where they are?" The mother was impatient. She shouted, "Old woman, bring the children to me. My breasts are full of milk. They are hurting." The old woman said, "I have been working on a net bag. My eyes are not good and I have just stayed here. I haven't been watching the children." The mother looked and looked and looked for them. She couldn't find them.

Then she went to the garden to get food. She brought it back to the village but she did not cook it. She was thinking about her children. And her breasts were very tight and uncomfortable. She looked and looked for the children. "If I don't find my children I will kill you." This is what she said to the old woman. Then she went into the old woman's house to look. She lifted a pandanus mat and looked under it. But the children weren't there. The old woman said, "I don't know where the children are. I could not watch them. I do not see well." Then the mother saw the plank. She saw spit on it. She thought, "Spit doesn't appear on a plank that way." She didn't look at it but she wondered.

The mother and father got all sorts of gifts together. They collected all sorts of goods—many shells and other things. They put them by the plank. Then they waited. They were quiet and waited and watched. The old woman wanted to take the gifts for herself. She went to the plank. She lifted it up and discovered the children under the plank. They had rotted. The spirit of the plank said, "I covered the children this way. I covered them." This is the story of planks killing children. They were not looked after well and the plank fell on them and killed them. The mother and father gave pay to the maternal relatives. Then the children were burned and the plank was split into firewood with a stone adze and put in the sun to dry. The old woman in this story wasn't punished.

As I said, almost any village child has more people taking care of it than does a child who grows up in Kainantu, where there are usually no relatives of either the father or the mother. The child is held and taken care of only by his father and mother, his brothers and sisters. Sometimes a friend of the parents may help but they don't take care of it for very long, just for a short while. In Kainantu the child is with its mother most of the time, much more than it is in the village. It is also with its father and brothers and sisters much more when it is young. A child in Kainantu does not know as many people when it is growing up. It is close to its own immediate family.

My children are different not only from village children but, in some ways, from each other. Paulo and Yebi and the first Simi spent much more time out in the village than have my other children. When I worked for you the first time, they spent a great deal of time at Abiera. Also, Paulo and Yebi would go to Abiera more when they were babies. Some of Paulo's feasts were held there. When these three children went to Abiera, people would tell them, "So and so is your mother's brother," or "So and so is your grandmother," or "So and so is your mother." They would tell them this so Paulo, Yebi, and the first Simi knew more people at Abiera. They knew how the different people were related to them and they felt well acquainted with many people. The three children felt that they really knew their relatives and they felt free to be friendly with them.

My younger children have spent much less time in the village. They do not know the village people well nor do they feel comfortable with them. Hinda never likes to go to the village. But she is different from my other children in many ways. She doesn't like to share her things with other children, even in Kainantu. She is even more this way in the village. When Anto came to Abiera with me the people were very good to her. They told her who all the people were and how they were related to her. But she did not feel very free with them, even those who were close relatives. The ones who come into Kainantu often, the people who come to our house when they come there, these my children know well. But there are not very many of them compared to how many people there are in the whole village. I think that the second Simi and Wanama are learning more about people in the village. But Wanama wants to stay with me all the time. She does not like to be away from me very long.

As you know, Simi was out here for several months. But he did not fit in very well with the children here. He was an outsider who attracted a lot of attention. He was a big show-off. The village children liked to watch him and hang around him. But he couldn't really play with them. He chased them a lot and hit them with sticks. He did not want to play with them at their games. He is now living in Kainantu and happy to be there. He does miss me though, and that is why Paulo brought him out here on the bicycle last week. It was to see me. But he likes living in Kainantu better than living out in the village. My children are Station children. They have grown up away from the village. They don't know their relatives very well. They can't speak Tairora. They are more used to Robaga and me and their brothers and sisters. And they feel closer to some of our friends in Kainantu than they do to some of their close relatives in the village.

I had this dream last night. I wanted to cross a river. It wasn't really water. There were stones but they were very big stones. Much bigger than you really see in the rivers around here. They were as big as a Jeep. I went to the water, it was good water. Clean water. There was no dirt in it. The stones were big. Some of them were as big as a bus. I wanted to cross the water but I couldn't. I took hold of the big stone. The water took me and I moved on. I came to a place where there was a lot of grass. It was clean, as if a machine had cleaned it. There was no rubbish or litter around. There were big roads all round. Many, many big roads. The stone was as big as a bus. I came to a house. It was a house like some houses on the coast. I thought, "Is this a house for eating?" I thought I would see Simi here. I thought I would see my first Simi, the one who died. I didn't think I was sleeping. I thought I really saw all this. My eyes were really looking at all this. There were three cars altogether. And a bus full of people. The people didn't talk. They just looked. I was outside. I held on to the bus. I saw big water. How was I to get across it? "Shall I go back?" I thought. "Should I let go?" The bus carried me through the water. I wasn't afraid of the water. I saw the house again. "Should I go back now? No, I've crossed. I'll see Simi first." I looked and looked but I didn't see him. Then I woke up.

Wanama was sleeping between Ihube and me. Ihube didn't cover her up and she got cold. She cried. She wanted to get up and pee. She was hungry and wanted to eat. So I got up. Then I told them, Ihube and Boha, that I had seen a really good place. I saw a lot of houses with metal roofs and some with sago palm thatch roofs. They were houses on the coast. I told them that I had looked and looked for Simi. I looked all over. But I didn't see him.

I have already told you about some of the ways my children differ from children in the villages. There are many ways in which all the children who live in Kainantu are different from those who live out in the villages. Children whose fathers work for the government—policemen, doctors' aides, store helpers, teachers— come from many different areas in New Guinea and they are different from village children. For one thing, they are not punished as severely. In the villages children are not punished very often, but when they are they are often hurt quite a bit. Parents hit them with sticks. They also box them on the ears or the head or on their back, and they hit them hard. Station children are hit more on their hands or legs or buttocks.

The doctors and nurses tell us never to hit the children on the ears or on the head. They say that is very bad for a child. Also they tell us not to hit the children with large sticks. I think we punish our children as often as children in the village are punished, but we don't hit them on the ears the way village people do, we don't hurt them as much.

Most of the children in Kainantu don't know about the places from which their mothers and fathers came. Many of them have lived only at government stations. Some of them have never been to their parents' villages, others have visited their parents' villages but not for very long. Their "village" is Kainantu. That is the only one they know or the one they know best. There are a few children, like mine, who can go to their parents' villages sometimes, but not very many. All of my children have been to my village but not all of them have gone to Robaga's village. Only Paulo, Yebi, and the first Simi have been there.

Some children become so used to living at a government station that if their father wants to stop working for the government and return to his village to live, his children do not want to go with him. If they are old enough they can get a job elsewhere. But if they are young children they have to go with their parents. It is very hard for them to go to a village that is strange to them and to live there and to learn who all the people are. Even though many of the people are their relatives and will be good to them, the children don't know these people. It is hard for the children to leave a government station and go back to their father's village. But this sometimes happens.

Most children who grow up at government stations don't like the villages. They don't like the native style of clothing, all the dirt and filth of the villages or the houses, and all the bugs that are in them. You know how my children complained about the fleas and lice in Waraara's house when we first came out to Abiera. They were bitten a lot and they didn't like it. They are not used to bugs and dirt the way village children are. Children from Kainantu usually don't fit in well with village children. They haven't learned the same games and don't know how to play with village children. Station boys haven't grown up playing with the bow and arrow as village boys have, so they don't know how to play with it when they go out to the village and they don't think it is much fun. They learn about the guitar and ukulele and like to play them. But village boys don't know anything about that. Kainantu boys also play basketball and softball and the boys in the village don't. And the little girls in Kainantu play with dolls and learn to make clothes for them. But village girls don't. So children from Kainantu don't like to live in the villages.

Children in Kainantu don't have as much free time to run around as children in the village do. At the station children spend more time in organized work at home. They go to school for a certain part of the day. When they come home they have set chores to do. Then, after they eat their evening meal they must study their school lessons. Village children do some work but it doesn't make much difference when they do it. A boy or girl knows that he or she must fetch water and collect firewood. But as a rule they can get it when they feel like it or when their mother asks them to do it. There is no set time when they have to do it every day.

In Kainantu boys and girls don't play together as much as they do in the village either. There are playgrounds for girls and playgrounds for boys. They don't play on the same ones. Older boys play cricket and Rugby. They also play on soccer teams. Boys play these games even more now than they used to. There are more teams. And they hope that they can become very good and go to Wau or Goroka or other places to play the teams there. Then the best team in New Guinea plays Papua. The Papuans usually win. They are better because they play against the Australians more than the New Guineans do. Also they have been playing these games for many more years and they know more about them.

Boys and girls, men and women play basketball. The teams, both kinds, travel around the country for games. They go to Wau or Lae or Goroka in July and August. They go to Madang last, usually at Christmas time. Men and women play and both teams travel. The women's team from Wau is the best. They even have some older women on it and they don't get out of breath when they play basketball. If I were as old as Baitaj and I tried to play basketball I would be out of breath right away. But the Wau women don't get out of breath. They are very good basketball players.

In Kainantu we take baths in the river the way the people do at the village. That is, those people in the village who do take baths. As you know, many people in the village never take a bath at all and in earlier times this was true of everybody. When the weather is hot and someone has been working very hard in the garden he or she might want to wash off in the river, but it was not common. Today some village people do take baths as do we and although we bathe more often we do it in the same way as the village people. However, in Kainantu men use one part of the river and women use another. They never go to the same place but keep to their own part of the river for bathing. In the village, though, men and women go to the same place. In Kainantu even brothers and sisters are separated when they get to be twelve or so. It is all right for little children to bathe together in either place. But boys and girls are separated from each other much earlier in Kainantu than they are in the village. In Kainantu we wash and bathe often. We also brush our teeth. No one in the village does that. We wet the brush in a cup of water. Then, after we brush we spit the water into a basin that we later empty.

I think that children in Kainantu mind their parents much better than those in the village. They are not such bigheads as the village children are. They don't sass their parents as much as village children do. Kainantu children go to school, come home from school, and help with the work, as well as playing. Girls are better taken care of too. They cannot run around as freely as they can at the village. Parents tell their daughters not to be familiar with the boys. They are told not to get pregnant, told not to disgrace their parents' name. At Kainantu when a boy and girl like each other they exchange pictures, rings, and things like that. If they are going to school at different places they write letters to each other.

Boys and girls have parties at their parents' houses and they often dance. They dance like the Australians. They don't dance like the villagers do. They don't like that kind of dancing, just the Australian kind of dancing. You know how we dance. It is not like the Australians, one man and one woman dancing together, looking at each other and holding hands. In the village a lot of people dance alone, some of them carry their drums, beat their drums. Other dancers in the village can form a line and dance that way, one following the other. In the village, too, we sing while we dance. The White man doesn't do this.

Most parents look after their children well. And they tell the girls to be careful of the boys. Nomi's daughter, who was in school with Yebi, got pregnant by a man from Manus. He left Kainantu soon after that. She had the baby and then married a Kamano man. She is still married to him. I was cross with her about it all. About her getting pregnant before she was married. Getting pregnant by the Manus man. I said to her, "Why didn't you wait? You could have married Paulo and then Yebi could have married your brother. That would have been a good exchange. You should have waited. Didn't you want to marry. Paulo? But you can't do that now. You're like a dog that comes back and smells shit." That's what I said to her. I was cross with her because I thought it would have been a good marriage exchange.

We do not exchange brothers and sisters in marriage as much as we used to. But I think it is a good thing and that would have been a good exchange. I don't think Robaga cared though. He would rather have his children marry people from the coast or other areas rather than people from around here. Bulolo, Wau, Sepik, Madang—all those places are all right. But I don't think he wants his children to marry people from around Kainantu.

Did I tell you that Paulo now has a job with the malaria control unit? He goes on patrol with the doctor and spends most of his time away from Kainantu. They take blood from people so they can tell how many people have malaria. I hope he stays with his job. He is lazy and does not like to work. He just likes to be dressed up all the time and show off. His father spoils him and gives him money for things. He doesn't work much himself to earn money. Maybe though he will stay at this job. I hope so. He quit school in the fourth grade although he could have gone all through school. He would not finish as Yebi is doing. Robaga and I wanted him to but he is very lazy. He can read and write English a little bit but not as well as Yebi. He can't read much better than Robaga can. They both read the letters that Yebi sends to us from Lae where she goes to school. Both of them can read the letters that you will write to us too.

There are many ways that people who live in Kainantu are different from village people. But there are ways that they are alike. Some of them have stories just as we have stories. Here is one story that I heard from coastal people who were living in Kainantu. A man went to work for a Master called Eara. The man worked for Eara for a long while. He worked and worked but he was never paid. He didn't even get one shilling. He just worked and worked, all the time. After he had served his time he said, "I have finished my period of work now. I would like to be paid. I want to go back to my village and see my relatives." Eara gave him some money but it was not enough. The man was dissatisfied. He didn't like it at all. The Master gave him laplaps. He didn't like that. The Master got all kinds of things and gave them to the man but he was not satisfied. Then he gave him a ring, a ring to wear on his finger. The man took the ring. He left. He didn't say anything. He just left with the ring.

Then he got a cat and a cockatoo. He treated them as if they were two children of his. He took them and he left. He walked and walked. He looked at the ring a lot. He turned the ring. Then food, a plate, spoon, many things appeared from nowhere. He got them for nothing. Then he rubbed the ring and everything disappeared. Wild cat and cockatoo stayed with him. At one place the man wanted to sleep. He rubbed the ring and a house appeared with many things in it. The man bathed, ate, and slept. At dawn he rubbed the ring again and everything disappeared. He walked and walked and walked. He came to one village where a lot of rats were policemen for a Master. The man slept. He slept with the Master. He took the ring off and put it on a table. The Master slept, too. At first he pretended to sleep. He took the ring and hid it. When the man awakened at dawn he could not find the ring. He looked for it but he could not find it. He was hungry and he had no food. He went in one direction and called out to the cat and the cockatoo. He said, "You go to all the police of this Master." They went to the rats. The cat caught a rat and held him and the cockatoo sat down on top of him. The rat said, "You can't hold me prisoner this way. I am a policeman." Wild cat said, "You look out or I'll eat you. You go inside and find the ring." All of them went inside but they could not find it. They just couldn't find it. (The Master had put it in his mouth.)

Then rat's spirit went into the Master's ear and then into his mouth where he found the ring. He brought it out and gave it to wild cat. Cockatoo said, "Give it to me. I fly in the air above things. It wouldn't be good for you to lose it on the ground." But wild cat was insistent. He walked on the ground and he wanted to keep the ring. The cockatoo said, "You walk on the ground." "Yes, I do," said wild cat. Then wild cat crossed a stream. The ring fell into the mouth of a fish. Wild cat tried to find him but the fish didn't come back. Cockatoo was very angry. He said, "What did I tell you?" He then reprimanded wild cat and went away. The cockatoo went to the Master and talked to him.

Then the cat turned around and walked and walked back to the Master's place. He caught the rat again. Said some things to him. Told him to get some fish line from his Master. Wild cat took the line and fished in the water. He caught one fish. Cut its belly open.

No ring was in it. He caught another fish, cut its stomach open but found no ring. He caught many fish and looked inside each one of them but with no luck. Finally he caught the fish that had the ring in it. He told cockatoo that he had found it and cockatoo wanted the ring but wild cat wouldn't give it to him. So the cockatoo went to the Master and told him. The two went after the cat.

They met a big *masalai,* a *masalai* that ate people—men, women, and children. He would devour all people. People sometimes gave other people to the *masalai* to keep him from attacking them. Eara, the Master, dressed a child in his best clothes and ornaments and offered it to the *masalai* to eat. Then his wife was dressed up in her best finery and offered to the *masalai* for him to eat. The *masalai* lived in the forest. The table in his house was always covered with blood from all the people he had eaten. The Master said to him, "You eat these two people (the child and the woman) and you can eat me too." The *masalai* had two heads. The *masalai* moved his biggest head and a big wind came up that made everybody shiver. The *masalai* came nearer. He looked at the White woman who was all dressed up in her best clothes and jewelry. The *masalai* was very happy and he was licking his chops over the thought of eating her.

The Master's dog was sleeping near the door. The Master held a large black palm stick in his hands and he waited. He was holding it tightly and waiting. The *masalai* looked at the child, at the woman, at the Master. He stopped to rest and catch his breath. He was happy in anticipation of the feast he was going to have. He wanted to eat all three people at one time. As the *masalai* drew near, the dog pushed a stick at his balls. Then Eara jumped up and got his stick. He bashed one of the heads of the *masalai*. The other one he broke with another black palm stick. The Master killed the *masalai*. Then all of the policemen came to eat the blood of the *masalai*. The rats rubbed the blood on their guns.

The Master then went to his house. Goods and lots of things just appeared from nowhere. Then the Master rubbed the ring and a ship appeared out of nowhere. The ship was decorated. A black flag was hanging from it and they took it down. The ship has come now. The Master rubbed the ring and everything of his appeared, food, houses, everything that anyone could want. "Master killed the *masalai*. You people didn't kill him. Master killed the *masalai*. You are just rats. Nothing more. You didn't kill him."

I have told you that station children differ from village children. Many children in Kainantu know nothing about village life. They have never seen their parents' villages. The life of the big people is also very different from that in the village. Many of the people at the station were born in other parts of Papua New Guinea and they now live far from their villages. Living in Kainantu makes a big difference in their lives. The things they do, the work they do, the way they live, all are quite different from what they once knew. Most of them are not as lucky as I am. I have all the good things of living at the station yet I am still near where I grew up. I am near my relatives and old friends. I can come out to the villages to see them and many of them come to see me in Kainantu.

Here are some of the differences between Kainantu and the villages. One thing that has changed a lot is the way we dress. Most people in the villages still dress in the old fashion, the way our ancestors dressed. Women and girls wear skirts made of strips of bark. Men and older boys wear a belt with some bark strips hanging over their private parts. All of them are bare above the waist. Little boys go naked. Some men now wear laplaps if they can get the cloth, if they have the money to buy them at the trade stores. That is the way it is in the villages.

In Kainantu everyone wears Western clothes, cloth clothes. Shirts and trousers or shorts or laplaps for men and boys, blouses and laplaps or skirts for women and girls. A few men wear shoes but many men and most women still go barefoot as village people do. Shoes do not feel good on our feet. Some children wear them.

When the White man came, the missionaries especially wanted local people to wear their kind of clothes but most people could not get them. They wanted people to be better covered from the waist down and they wanted women to be all covered. They did not want to look at women's teats. Some of the missionaries had long white dresses for women. They would try to get women to buy them. Some of them would get them for when they were baptized. Other missionaries wanted laplaps and blouses. For men, just a laplap was thought best at first, but now many men wear trousers and shorts although some like laplaps. In Kainantu you can still see people who are naked from the waist up, but they don't live there. They have come in from their villages. Come in for court, or to sell potatoes or cabbages, or go to the doctor.

The clothes worn in the village, the clothes my people have worn since they were put on earth, can't be washed. They just get very dirty and are never washed. But the clothes we wear in Kainantu can be washed and we wash them in the river. We buy soap at the trade stores and use that to wash clothes as well as for washing our bodies. People in the villages are still very dirty, but in Kainantu we know how to keep our bodies and our clothing clean. We keep our houses clean too.

We always get the same rations and pay in Kainantu. There are no changes from week to week. When village men work for Masters they might get paid the proper ration or they might not. Some Masters, especially in the early days, gave very small rations. And they often paid less for things, food and work, than they should. You remember I told you about the time a Master paid me only one shilling for a large bag of sweet potatoes. I had carried the potatoes in my net bag a long way, several miles, from Kainantu to his plantation. He paid me one shilling. But that was a long time ago.

In Kainantu we are nearer the doctor if we get sick. And we are not afraid of him. We know he will not harm us and what he does for us, the medicine he gives us, is good for us. Many village people are still afraid to go to the doctor. Many of them don't want to walk to Kainantu to see him. They just have someone in the village treat them with our old ways of curing. Or they may go to a medical orderly when he travels through the area. But he can't do all the things the doctor can do.

In Kainantu we don't have to share everything with other people as we do in the village. What is our is ours. We help each other sometimes and we exchange things at certain times of the year.

But we don't have to share everything with other people. In the village you have to. Many things that we have here in Kainantu we can't share. If you give me your radio when you leave, this will belong to Robaga and me. We will let other people listen to it at our house but we don't have to do that. Only if we want to. We don't have to let anyone take it from our house to some other house. In the village there is a great deal of sharing.

In Kainantu a man can have only one wife. There are still a few men who have more than one wife, but only one of them can live in Kainantu with him. The other one stays in her husband's village. She may not see her husband very often. At one time Akro had two wives, one in Kainantu and one at Ontabura. That was a long time ago. His wife, Eto, is a strong woman and she made him get rid of the other wife.

There are other things that are different. We can go to court more easily than people in the village. They have to walk for miles. And very important is the school. All our children can go to school and those that finish can go on to school in Lae or Goroka if they want to. Some day village children may be able to go to school, but not now. I think all of my children will go to school here and finish. I hope that they go on further too, and I think they will. Paulo might not. He is such a bighead and so lazy that I don't know how far he will go. He can read and write English a little bit and he thinks that is enough for him to know.

In Kainantu there is church at ten o'clock on Sunday morning. Both the Seven Days and the Lutherans. Sometimes they are also held in the evening. Not many people go. People can be baptized in the churches. All my children except the two little ones have been baptized. The two small ones don't have sin yet. Also some people get married at a church. They get a marriage ticket to prove this. I do not go to church, because Robaga forbids it. But I have been baptized, as you know. I believe I am good enough that my spirit will go to heaven.

Another big difference between life in Kainantu and in the village is that there is less violence here. Big fights like long ago could never happen—fights between villages. The police would stop it.

Also, most men treat their wives better than they used to and better than many village men do. The *kiap* has told us for a long time that men should not beat their wives. They should be good to them and to their children too. Not many men beat their wives and for those who do, the beatings are not as brutal. The *kiap* tells the village men this too but they do not always listen to what he says. It is better now than it was but there are still bad beatings in the villages.

You remember the time Amata beat his wife—when we were living at Abiera. At first they yelled at each other. Then they pushed and slapped a bit. Then Amata grabbed a piece of two-by-four and began to hit her with it. He hit and hit and hit. We couldn't see them because they were inside the house. But we could hear the wood landing on her body. We heard her screams. He hit her mainly on the arms and back. It is a wonder her bones weren't broken. But you saw how swollen, black, and limp her arms were for days afterward. How bent over her back was. She could hardly walk.

She didn't take the case to court, because the *kiap* still doesn't do much against village men who beat their wives. But he does tell men in Kainantu, men who work for the government and the trade stores, that it is bad to beat a wife. If a man does, he may have to go to court. The *kiap* sends some of those who go to court, to jail. A Kamano woman would not sleep with her husband. He said to her, "So I'm not good enough for you," and then he cut her cunt. Then he set fire to her pubic hair with a match and she was burned. The *kiap* put the man in jail for two years. That was a long time to be in jail.

Do you remember the story I told you about Ekao? I told you about this a long time ago. It is about something that happened, something I saw when I was a little girl. You know that we believe that when a girl gets married she is supposed to fuck only with her husband. It has always been that way with my people. Some women didn't behave well though, they would fuck with other men—some with one or two, some with many. One time, when I was about eight years old, Apam and I went to the garden to get some old dead reeds to make a fire. In those days we saved the best wood for big fires, but we always had some old dry reeds around for small fires, or for starting big fires, or for warming ourselves when it was cold.

This day we were going out to get some of these old dry reeds, for there weren't any more at the house. While we were at the garden we noticed that men were coming from different directions and going to the woods at Bahiora. There were only men—no boys or girls or women—and they all had their bows and arrows. The men came alone or two at a time, not a lot at once. But they were all going in the direction of Bahiora. We tried to follow them to see what was going to happen. We didn't walk on the main paths but tried to keep out of sight of the men, because we didn't know what they were going to do and we wanted to watch them but we didn't want to get caught and punished. Children are not supposed to spy on their elders and girls particularly were not supposed to know what the men were doing. But we were curious, so we followed them.

When we got to where we could see them, for they were all in one place in the woods, we hid and remained very quiet so no one would know that we were there. There was only one woman there, one who had been brought there by her husband. When we arrived several men were holding her, and she was struggling and trying to get away from them.

It was Ekao, a young woman who did not like her husband so she slept not only with him but with other men as well. Her husband knew about it and he was angry with her. Three times when he caught her with another man he punished her in the manner of our ancestors by shooting an arrow into her thigh. You have seen the scars on her legs. Still Ekao did not behave properly and some of the other men, not only her husband, were disgusted with her for being so loose. They brought her to the woods where they were going to punish her. We were watching to see what happened.

First, all of the men fucked her, one after the other. Then they repeatedly hit various parts of her body with their genitals—they poked them in her ears, in her eyes, in her mouth, around her face, nose, all parts of her body—all of the men did. They didn't just penetrate her, they hit her and called her a lot of names. The men didn't shit or piss on her, just defiled her and hit her, and put their pricks all over her. Ekao screamed and yelled. The men tried to stop her by putting their hands over her mouth. They tried to restrain her. When she got tired she would quiet down, but again she would start struggling and shouting.

Some of the women who were working in their gardens heard her screams and they came running to the woods. When they saw what was happening they were very angry with the men and they began to yell at them. The men yelled back at the women and soon there was a big fight between the men and the women. They called each other names, they hit each other with their hands, and they even used sticks in the fight. Several people were hurt but no one was badly hurt. Some wounds bled, but the gashes were usually small and no one was hurt really seriously. Apam and I saw all this but the men and women didn't know we did. We were hidden in a good place and they did not discover us. After that Ekao remained faithful to her husband. She was a good wife. But she still has the scars on her legs from the arrow wounds that her husband gave to her earlier.

This could not happen today. Or could it?

Epilogue

I HAVE INDICATED THE RATHER SUCCESSFUL ACCULTURATIVE shift that Anyan made over a period of several decades. Dual processes were at work: on the one hand, she was relinquishing familiar cultural practices and values; on the other, she was acquiring and internalizing new, different, strange, cultural modes. Although there may have been some unhappy experiences during the metamorphosis, the changes basic to the cultural substitution occurring in Anyan's life were relatively equable. In her case, in contrast to the experience of many intercultural transients, a vital support seems always to have been in place—now in the old way of life, now in the new—as the attainment of one goal was superseded by another. The process to some extent was influenced, perhaps paced, by Anyan's desires.

It is intriguing to speculate that several motivating factors were at work as Anyan distanced herself from the village. With the birth of more children and the domestic demands of a growing family, one that within two decades would include six surviving children, the walking distance from Kainantu to Abiera became a deterrent of some power to active participation in village life. The logistics of returning even for special ceremonies became tedious.

This does not imply a lack of contact with the village. With increasing frequency Tairorans walked into Kainantu, and with some regularity visited Anyan at her house. In this manner she was able to maintain personal ties with friends and kin and to keep abreast of village news. Concurrently, as her children grew and became enmeshed in Station life, their mother's participation in local activities increased and she became more comfortable in the Euro–Pan Papua New Guinean culture of Kainantu.

This is not to suggest that Anyan encountered no difficulties as she made the transition from village to Station culture. But hers was not a single culture shock, not a single shift from one style to another, but rather an incremental cultural blend produced through time.

Slowly, Anyan's perception of the extra-Tairora world expanded to include other parts of the highlands as well as coastal Papua New Guinea. The former provided variations on a common cultural theme, modifications that occurred bit by bit on a geographical continuum.

The coast, on the other hand, represented a much greater contrast, both to local cultural elements and to those changes that resulted from a considerably more prolonged period of contact with Western culture than was true of the highlands. In a sense this was a third cultural ingredient in her odyssey. One could not walk to the coast. Riding in an airplane, a novel artifact, was in itself stressful. And having arrived there, one ate unpalatable foods such as sago, saw the ocean, large fish, and Chinese shopkeepers, rode in a boat or canoe, both of them frightening experiences, and had to endure a hot climate, which Anyan found exceedingly oppressive. Even things she was accustomed to, such as trade stores, produce markets, government offices and storage facilities, not to mention the quality of housing for local residents, were on a much greater scale than her familiar haunts in the highlands.

Anyan was aware of the difference between her cultural cocoon and her children's. In contrast to their mother, having grown up in the Euro–Pan Papua New Guinean milieu, from their earliest years her children were at home there. Anyan recognized the potential for their continued progression toward immersion in Western culture through the formal education they were privileged to receive. She hoped that some of them would become teachers, that some of them would work for the government, that some of them might be ranchers or their wives. Whether she envisioned that some of them would venture as far from Papua New Guinea as Australia, I do not know.

In 1964, after two decades of living on the outside, although at times she was a bit nostalgic for some aspects of village life and she maintained relationship ties to villagers, Anyan was truly ensconced in the local Euro–Pan Papua New Guinean culture at the government station, Kainantu.

Some evenings she would come in to converse with us, preferring to talk about things of "global" importance rather than the details of village life that occupied us during the day. At these times she sat on a chair (she and I always sat on the ground in the village or gardens). Anyan was one of the few locals we knew who were at ease on these crude wooden contraptions of Western origin.

One evening she wondered aloud why Europeans had come to Papua New Guinea, especially why they came to the highlands. She acknowledged that Tairora do not know, really, why the Westerners came, what prompted their arrival. Anyan's hypothesis was that their own land was not very good and they were often short of food. In their search for new land they came to the highlands, where they found much good ground. This was Anyan's own thinking; admittedly she had no way of assessing its correctness.

That Anyan accepted the changes in her life without rancor or regret indicates, as I have suggested elsewhere, that the gradual relinquishment of Tairora culture and the acceptance of a Papua New Guineaized Western replacement was not traumatic. Forced adjustments had to be made—diet, cleanliness, clothing, a foreign system of justice with its courts and jails, to name a few. Other changes, such as participation in village-oriented activities, permitted choice. The Euro–Pan Papua New Guinean culture she embraced represented the end of a fairly successful journey, and by the time of her death in the early seventies, it described her place in the world.[10]

Glossary

Agarabi—northern neighbors of the Tairora.

Bamboo tube—a section of bamboo trunk in which all of the nodes except the lowest have been removed. Uses vary from carrying water to cooking food on the open hearth.

Big Man—an outstanding local leader.

Cargo Cult—a millenarian movement common in Melanesia. Simply, it is an attempt to acquire goods of Western origin through magical means. (See notes.)

Catechist—a New Guinean in charge of a mission station.

Dracaena—a tropical plant whose colorful leaves are used in a variety of ways from boundary markers to personal decoration.

Gadsup—neighbors of the Tairora to the northeast.

Hampu—a ritual performed by males to lure the lover of one of them from her village.

Indicate—roughly, betrothed.

Kamano—western neighbors of the Tairora.

Kiap—a government officer, often a patrol officer. In the early years of Western contact the local people sometimes included the constabulary—New Guineans from the coast—in this term.

Kudzu—a plant, *Pueraria,* whose tough stems have many uses as rope.

Laplap—a wraparound skirt worn by men and women.

Lucky—*Laki* in Tok Pisin, a card game used for gambling, similar to "21."

Luluai—a local leader appointed by the government; his badges of office are a distinctive cap and a medal worn on a chain around the neck.

Masalai—bush spirit; demon.

Mata—European man.

Matoto—the preeminent Tairora Big Man in the decades immediately preceding Western contact. His exploits and power were known over a large area.

Missis—European woman.

Pidgin—See Tok Pisin.

Pitpit—commonly *Setaria palmifolia;* reeds with multiple uses ranging from fencing material to kindling. Edible pitpit is *Saccharum edule.*

Sago—sago palm, *Metroxylon,* the starchy pith of which is a staple food among people living on the coast of Papua New Guinea.

Tanim tok—an interpreter.

Tin—snuff tin used as a purse to carry small items.

Tok Pisin—a national language of Papua New Guinea; earlier called Melanesian Pidgin or Pidgin English. Used in interlanguage communication.

Tultul—a government-appointed local official with cap and medal to signify status; second in command to *luluai,* often chosen because of some facility with Tok Pisin.

Win—"wind"; associated with Cargo Cult.

Winged bean—*Psophocarpus tetragonolobus;* a plant with edible fruits, leaves, and roots.

Notes

1. In 1953, James B. Watson and I, with our infant daughter Anne, arrived in New Guinea for a year and a half of anthropological fieldwork in the eastern section of the island's central highlands. During this sojourn, financed by the Ford Foundation of New York, we resided in three different villages, two of them Tairora (J. Watson 1992).

A decade later the three of us, with young son Jim, spent a year in New Guinea, our time divided between two Tairora villages, one of which was the village in which Anyan had grown up. The 1963–64 field experience was part of the University of Washington Micro-evolution Project, an interdisciplinary study among four local groups that spoke separate although related languages: Auyana (Robbins 1982), Awa, Gadsup (duToit 1974), and Tairora (J. Watson 1983). Disciplines involved in addition to ethnography were linguistics (McKaughan 1973), physical anthropology (Littlewood 1972), human geography (Pataki-Schweitzer 1980), psychological anthropology (Leininger 1966), and archaeology (V. Watson and Cole 1977). This multidisciplinary undertaking, spanning almost a decade, was financed by the National Science Foundation of Washington, D.C.

2. Tairora myths and stories tend to be within the purview of men, not women. The more common myths are shared, but the details in a version that a woman relates are meager compared with those of a man's. The stories included in this account were from the male reservoir filtered through Anyan's retelling.

Sometimes when she arrived at our house in the morning she would be eager to recount a piece of Tairora lore so I could record it in my notebook before we began our own project for the day. A puzzling aspect of the exercise was Anyan's inability to elaborate

184

or clarify some of the details of a story. A case in point is my request for further information about the "skull man."

I soon learned that Anyan's father, wishing to share his considerable knowledge of local lore, for the first time told some of the myths and stories to his daughter. He intended that she serve as intermediary between a venerated Tairora elder and the field anthropologist.

3. The central highlands of Papua New Guinea, as the country is now called, were isolated from the influence of Western culture well into the twentieth century. Although the eastern and northeastern fringes of the easternmost highlands were penetrated by a few missionaries and miners in the 1920s, it was not until 1932 that a formal Western political presence, the Upper Ramu Patrol Post, was established. This later became the town of Kainantu, often referred to as the "government station" or just "station." Thus 1930 is a convenient date to use for the opening of the highlands.

Although the intrusion of Western influence was tentative at first, it gained momentum, especially after the end of World War II. In short, a series of autonomous groups of people, speaking a variety of languages and often feuding with one another, under Western, mainly Australian, influence began to be forged into a single political entity. At the time of our fieldwork New Guinea was a United Nations Trust Territory administered by Australia.

The government official known as the *kiap* (see Glossary), headquartered in Kainantu, was responsible for extending, and then maintaining, Western law and order in the region. Although an Assistant District Officer might be in charge of a government station such as Kainantu, patrol officers were common functionaries directly involved in exploring the rather large region, unknown to Westerners, taking a census in the many villages, introducing Western medical practices, and ensuring the maintenance of peace as it was established over ever-larger numbers of feuding groups.

4. Tropical ulcers and scabies were among the most common diseases with which pre-contact highlanders had to contend. Two of the most dreaded diseases were yaws and leprosy. Although

they share some similarities, such as the disintegration of body parts, their etiologies differ. In speaking of the individuals we knew who had saddle nose, or who lacked nasal tip and alae or lips, Anyan spoke consistently of yaws. The "cure" of yaws was one of the more "miraculous" results of introduced Western medicine. With a seemingly magical injection by a medical orderly, progress of the disease was arrested although the disfigurement remained.

5. Although World War II impinged on the Papua New Guinea highlands, it is difficult to assess the extent of its effect on the Tairora. The abandonment of the government station at Kainantu by Western officials may have been a bit unsettling even though a more inclusive foreign presence, the Australian New Guinea Administrative Unit, retained some control in the highlands. Japanese soldiers did penetrate the highlands but by no means in numbers similar to those on the coast, nor was their threat as real.

Eventually Western control was restored at the local level in Kainantu. At least two results of this disruption can be envisaged for the Tairora and their neighbors. The absence of strict control permitted the temporary abandonment of some newly introduced practices and a return to past local behavior. Second, the opportunity arose to see artifacts of Western culture not fully known before, such as airplanes that had crashed.

6. *Hampu* is a ceremony performed by a male, and several of his age-mates, to attract the attention of a female with whom he would like to elope, thus avoiding such obstacles as parental permission and marriage payments. Gathering on a hill or mountain at some distance from the village in which the girl resides, they follow certain procedures such as singing love songs to be heard only by the girl, and digging a large hole and filling it with wood to produce a fire whose smoke will not only be visible to the girl but will have the power to entice her away from her village. In earlier times *hampu* was often practiced by people who lived in villages that were feuding with one another.

7. Dreams serve several functions for Tairora, such as suggesting future happenings, indicating possible sorcery, and placing the dreamer in a situation of contact with his or her spirit. To be most

effective, a dream should be recounted to another person as soon as possible after the dreamer awakens. Effectiveness varies: some dreams are soon forgotten but others may even form the basis for songs powerful enough to become embedded in Tairora lore. (J. Watson 1983:287 ff.)

8. A variety of millenarian movements in reaction to the introduction of Western culture and its bearers were common in Melanesia. They were labeled Cargo Cults (cargo being the generic term for goods of Western origin). Objects such as clothing, tools, canned food, and guns, especially if they arrived by ship with no apparent effort on the part of the recipients, constituted cargo. A typical response of the local residents was the belief that if certain prescriptions were set in place and certain proscriptions heeded, Western goods would come to them as if by magic.

Cargo responses in the highlands were generally less elaborated than those in coastal areas. The Tairora of my acquaintance experienced at least two manifestations of the movement, separated by an interval of several years. Participants in the activity need not include all members of a community. Although the details of cargo activity might vary from village to village, there were certain common themes: a belief in a supernatural force, the "win," that caused participants to shiver and shake; the construction of a special meeting house; the manufacture of wooden replicas of firearms to be used in simulated military drills; the slaughter of large numbers of pigs; and the consumption of garden produce with no thought given to replacement. In time, as the hoped for acquisitions did not materialize, the enthusiasm and belief dissipated.

9. Since the data in this volume were recorded, many political and social changes have occurred in the country about which I write. What was then the Trust Territory of New Guinea, administered for the United Nations by Australia, has, together with Papua, achieved independent status in the world community as the country of Papua New Guinea. The date of this landmark occurrence was 1975. But for over a decade prior to that time, innovations in the political structure of the country were moving it in the direction of self-rule. Local councils were established to oversee

matters of law and order among smaller social units, originally with more or less autonomy, some of which was maintained under Western governmental rule. Equally innovative was the whole process of establishing voting rights and prerogatives. Not only was the act of voting itself a radical cultural introduction, but the fact that it was a countrywide—national, if you will—selection of individuals to represent heterogeneous groups in the capital at Port Moresby was a conceptual breakthrough. Since becoming independent, Papua New Guinea has experienced rather great changes, including increased facilities for commercial activities, education, and health.

10. Sometime after we left Papua New Guinea, Anyan bore her ninth child, a son, since deceased. Anyan herself died in the early 1970s. Robaga, who survived her by almost two decades, continued to guide and care for the children through their college years. The six surviving children, grown to adulthood, are now established in the independent nation of Papua New Guinea, all but one of them continuing to reside in the highlands. The eldest daughter is a Provincial Nursing Officer; the second is a teacher, married to the headmaster of a primary school; the third teaches high school, and her husband is employed by the federal government in the nation's capital; and the youngest daughter and her husband are both hospital nurses. Of the sons, one works for the National Broadcasting Commission and the other is a hospital ambulance driver. There are twenty-one grandchildren.

Supplementary Reading

Berndt, Ronald M.
  1962 *Excess and Restraint: Social Control among a New Guinea Mountain People.* Chicago: University of Chicago Press.
duToit, Brian M.
  1974 *Akuna: A New Guinea Village Community.* Rotterdam: A. A. Balkema.
Hays, Terence E., ed.
  1992 *Ethnographic Presents: Pioneering Anthropologists in the Papua New Guinea Highlands.* Berkeley: University of California Press.
Leininger, Madeleine M.
  1964 "A Gadsup Village Experiences Its First Election." *Journal of the Polynesian Society* 73:205–9.
  1966 "Convergence and Divergence of Human Behavior: An Ethnopsychological Comparative Study of Two Gadsup Villages in the Eastern Highlands of New Guinea." Ph.D. dissertation, University of Washington, Seattle.
Lindenbaum, Shirley
  1979 *Kuru Sorcery: Disease and Danger in the New Guinea Highlands.* Mountain View, Calif.: Mayfield Publishing Company.
Littlewood, Robert A.
  1972 *Physical Anthropology of the Eastern Highlands of New Guinea.* Seattle: University of Washington Press.
McKaughan, Howard P., ed.
  1973 *The Languages of the Eastern Family of the East New Guinea Highland Stock.* Seattle: University of Washington Press.
Pataki-Schweizer, K. J.
  1980 *A New Guinea Landscape: Community, Space, and Time in the Eastern Highlands.* Seattle: University of Washington Press.

Radford, Robin

   1987   *Highlanders and Foreigners in the Upper Ramu: The Kainantu Area, 1919–1942.* Carlton: Melbourne University Press.

Robbins, Sterling

   1982   *Auyana: Those Who Held onto Home.* Seattle: University of Washington Press.

Watson, James B.

   1963   "A Micro-Evolution Study in New Guinea." *Journal of the Polynesian Society* 72:188–92.

   1964   "A General Analysis of the Elections at Kainantu." *Journal of the Polynesian Society* 73:199–204.

   1965   "The Kainantu Open and South Markham Special Electorates." In *The Papua-New Guinea Elections 1964,* edited by David G. Bettison et al., pp. 91–119. Canberra: Australian National University Press.

   1971   "Tairora: The Politics of Despotism in a Small Society." In *Politics in New Guinea: Traditional and in the Context of Change, Some Anthropological Perspectives,* edited by Ronald M. Berndt and Peter Lawrence, pp. 224–75. Nedlands: University of Western Australia Press, 1971. Seattle: University of Washington Press, 1973.

   1983   *Tairora Culture: Contingency and Pragmatism.* Seattle: University of Washington Press.

   1992   "Kainantu: Recollections of a First Encounter." In *Ethnographic Presents: Pioneering Anthropologists in the Papua New Guinea Highlands,* edited by Terence E. Hays, pp. 167–98. Berkeley: University of California Press.

Watson, Virginia D.

   1965   "Agarabi Female Roles and Family Structure: A Study in Sociocultural Change." Ph.D. dissertation, University of Chicago.

   1979   "New Guinea Prehistory: A Model of Regional Comparison." *Archaeology and Physical Anthropology in Oceania* 14(2):83–98.

Watson, Virginia Drew, and J. David Cole

   1977   *Prehistory of the Eastern Highlands of New Guinea.* Seattle: University of Washington Press.

Index